LESS THAN TWO DOLLARS A DAY

Less Than Two Dollars a Day

*A Christian View of World Poverty
and the Free Market*

Kent A. Van Til

WILLIAM B. EERDMANS PUBLISHING COMPANY
GRAND RAPIDS, MICHIGAN / CAMBRIDGE, U.K.

Published 2007 by

Wm. B. Eerdmans Publishing Co.

2140 Oak Industrial Drive N.E., Grand Rapids, Michigan 49505 /

P.O. Box 163, Cambridge CB3 9PU U.K.

Printed in the United States of America

12 11 10 09 08 07   7 6 5 4 3 2 1

Library of Congress Cataloging-in-Publication Data

Van Til, Kent A.

Less than two dollars a day:

a Christian view of world poverty and the free market / Kent A. Van Til.

p.   cm.

Includes bibliographical references.

ISBN 978-0-8028-1767-9 (pbk.: alk. paper)

1. Poverty — Religious aspects — Christianity.

2. Free enterprise — Religious aspects — Christianity.

3. Distributive justice — Religious aspects — Christianity.

4. Wealth — Religious aspects — Christianity.

5. Economics — Religious aspects — Christianity.

I. Title.

BV4647.P6V36   2007

261.8'5 — dc22

2006036410

www.eerdmans.com

To my amigos
from Highland and Calvin
to San Jose, Brookfield, Marquette, and Hope

You have brought me blessings and joy.

Contents

CONTENTS

Contents

Acknowledgments

I should first acknowledge Mom and Dad, and businesspeople like John and Jay who showed me at a very early point that money is a tool for use in the Kingdom. Dr. Ted Minnema introduced me to this subject matter, and modeled the virtues of temperance and humility.

I also have the honor of acknowledging the Theology Department at Marquette University. Their doctoral program in "Theology and Society" gave me the opportunity to bring together economics, political theory, and theology in one program and one dissertation, from which this book is derived. The wisdom and erudition of my director — Christine Hinze — was matched only by her kindness. Dierdre Dempsey is not only a good tennis player but a great Hebrew scholar. John Davis, virtually a co-director, taught me economics in a way that even a theologian could understand. If every Protestant pastor/teacher could have a priest/professor like Fr. Thomas Hughson, S.J., the world would be a better place. And Dan Maguire was Dan.

Chapter Three, "Why the Poor Won't Necessarily Gain from the Free Market's Distribution," appeared in the *Journal of Markets & Morality* 7, no. 2 (Fall 2004): 441-66. Much of the material on Kuyper and Walzer appeared as "Abraham Kuyper and Michael Walzer: The Justice of the Spheres," in the *Calvin Theological Journal* 20, no. 2 (November 2005): 267-90.

ACKNOWLEDGMENTS

My doctorate was earned via the "sweat of the Frau," Kathy's. We didn't live on less than two dollars a day, but she and the girls made some sacrifices. Jen DeRuiter, a student at Hope College, did some low-cost but high-value copy editing. Finally, thanks to cousin, pal, and editor Reinder, who moved this project from academic treatise to book. My proceeds from this book will support Christian development projects in the Third World.

CHAPTER ONE

Distributing Earth's Benefits and Burdens

In the 1990s my wife and I worked and lived in Central America. Our three children were born there, and on many occasions (especially during long Midwestern winters) we get nostalgic about our friends and experiences there. While we lived there we had a maid by the name of Ester, a woman who was about our age and had three children of her own. But the similarities stopped there. Though she lived only a couple of miles away, her house was made of tin and had just gotten electricity. Ester was married, but if her husband ever came home, he was likely to abuse her. This abuse was but a continuation of the beatings her own mother had inflicted on her. Not only had her mother beaten her; she had also starved little Ester for days on end as a punishment for perceived misbehaviors. Though extremely bright and capable, Ester had been able to attend only six years of school before she was sent off to work full time. With Ester's help, her own children have done much better: one of them has graduated from college, the second is happily married, and the third is a craftsman. Even so, her children never had half the opportunities or material goods that our children have had.

Before moving to Central America, we had never known people who suffered as Ester did. Like us, our friends and family have been well fed and well treated. Nonetheless, Ester's story is far from unique. According to the World Development Indicators,[1] over 40 percent of the world's people live on less than two dollars a day. Across the world, 81 children out of 1,000 die before they reach the age of five; 100 million children do not attend primary school. More than a billion people lack access to safe water. The bad news goes on: little or no health service, lack of basic educational opportunities, mothers and children without basic nutrition, and so forth. By our standards, over 40 percent of the world's people lack basic necessities.

A quick look in the mirror reveals that, by comparison, you and I have been enormously privileged. I have never been hungry except for an occasional voluntary fast. I have received as much education as my capabilities permitted. Even while I was in college and graduate school, my income was far greater than two dollars per day. My children are well clothed, fed, and educated. My wife and I may argue, but no family member has ever struck another one. I have had wonderful, caring parents, not abusers. And I did not need to work full-time beginning in the sixth grade.

I also must admit that, in truth, I *earned* very few of these benefits. I did not work for all of my food, pay for all of my education, or invest wisely so that I could live comfortably. I *received* most of these things from parents, from society, and from schools or other institutions. The simplest explanation for the privileges I have received and the hardships that Ester has endured is that I was born in the United States of America and Ester was born in Panama: as a result of that accidental difference, I received many of the benefits of my society, and she received many of the burdens of her own.

It may be possible for some to stop at this point and say: "Yes, that's just how it is — some of us are born into relative privilege and others into relative hardship. Let's just get on with the hand we've been dealt." This book, however, will not stop at that point. Instead, it begins there. The contrast between Ester's life and mine — between those of us in the so-called First World and the poorest one-third of the world's people — is not simply a fact to accept; it is a problem to ad-

1. *World Development Indicators* (Washington: The World Bank, 2005), p. 4.

2

dress. In academic language, the heading under which this issue falls is "distributive justice." Reflection on this subject has a rich history; it has engaged men and women, Marxists and capitalists, ancients and moderns. In fact, it was the ancient Roman jurist Ulpian who coined a definition of distributive justice that is still in use: "Justice is the constant and perpetual desire to render each his due."[2] This long-standing definition of justice raises further questions: (1) Who is it that is due something? Everyone? My people? My family? My nation? (2) On what grounds or principles shall we determine that they are due things? Their needs? Their status? Their equality? Their achievements? Their relationship to me? Their citizenship? Their nature?

While answering all of these questions is beyond the scope of any one book, or perhaps any one person, in this book I will recommend a state of affairs in which distributive justice can actually occur. While my main focus will be the distribution of material goods, I recognize that other kinds of goods — such as education, clean air, access to medical care, and so forth — also form important parts of human life and must also be distributed justly. In addition to my experience in Latin America, the context for this book is shaped by two prominent realities: contemporary capitalist economy and the Christian faith. Since 1990, the former has been the uncontested victor in the long modern struggle between East and West, and it now serves as the process that guides the distribution of goods among the vast majority of the world's peoples. The latter is the Christian religious tradition that has shaped much of the world, and which guides me. In this book we will see how, at different points, these two realities relate, agree, and conflict.

In Scripture the problem of poverty arises no later than the book of Exodus. The poor Israelite slaves leave Egypt with the wealth of their former masters; they are then commanded to care for the poor, the widow, and the orphan in the land they received as a gift from

---

2. *Justicia est constans et perpetua voluntas jus suum cuique tribuendi,* in Giorgio del Vecchio, *Justice: An Historical and Philosophical Essay,* trans. Lady Guthrie (New York: Philosophical Library, 1953), p. 55.

God. In market economics, the poor are seen as those who live below a specific monetary standard. In this book I will often speak about poverty using the terms *basic human needs,* or *basic sustenance.* Defining these terms in a global context will be part of my task. Using Christian Scripture and traditions, I will argue that all humans merit access to basic sustenance because they all share God's image and God's world. Given the predominance of free-market economies in today's world, the next question that arises is: To what extent will the free market serve this particular demand of justice? In my attempt to answer that question, I will analyze the free-market system in light of its capability to meet basic human material needs, drawing on the resources of both ethics and economics.

Defining Terms

Before moving forward, I must define some terms. Because the language used in the landscape of justice can quickly become a thicket, some preliminary clarifications should help clear the path. When we speak of justice, there is a basic division between criminal justice and distributive justice. Criminal justice "distributes" punishments to those who have "earned" them by their actions; distributive justice, on the other hand, has to do with the distribution of society's benefits and burdens. In distinguishing between these two basic kinds of justice, philosopher Allen Buchanan says: "Theories of distributive justice attempt to articulate, order, and justify principles that specify distributions of benefits and burdens (other than punishments)."[3] Contemporary British political theorist David Miller provides a similar definition: "The subject matter of justice is the manner in which benefits and burdens are distributed among men (strictly, sentient beings) whose qualities and relationships can be investigated."[4] How we understand

---

3. Allen Buchanan, "Justice, Distributive," in Lawrence C. Becker and Charlotte B. Becker, eds., *Encyclopedia of Ethics* (London: Routledge, 2001), p. 920.

4. Miller, *Social Justice* (Oxford: Clarendon Press, 1976), p. 19.

"benefits and burdens" can be quite broad. It might include not only physical items and properties, but also opportunities for education, or duties such as military service and taxation, and so forth.

The principles that a theory of distributive justice attempts to "order, articulate and justify" relate to the basic issues underlying Ulpian's original definition.[5] Which characteristics of a person are relevant in a given distribution of benefits or burdens? And which principle of distribution applies to specific benefits and burdens?[6] To make this more concrete, let us consider the following example. We may say that candy should be distributed equally among all the children at a party. This simple statement establishes two principles for distribution: it provides the relevant characteristic of human beings who are eligible for distribution (only the children at this party) and also provides the grounds for distribution of the candy (equality). Such examples could be multiplied by changing the applicable characteristic of the recipient or the burden or benefit in question. For example, music scholarships shall be distributed to high-school students on the grounds of their musical proficiency shown in auditions. The quality of the students that makes them eligible for the benefit is the fact that they are high-school musicians, and the principle on which the distribution of the benefit will be based is their proficiency on an instrument.

If we have agreed that candy should be distributed to the children at the party on the grounds of equality, or that music scholarships should be distributed to high-school musicians on the basis of performance, we have granted rights to the children at the party and the musicians at the auditions. We would be unjust if we turned to one child and said, for instance, "Even though you are a child at this party, we will not give you candy because you have red hair, or you spilled your punch, or your father is greedy." Once we have set up the system in a certain way, people within it will have legitimate claims to the benefit or burden in question.

5. "Justice is the constant and perpetual desire to render each his due."
6. Buchanan, p. 920.

By setting up systems of justice in certain ways, we attempt to establish a state of affairs in which justice actually takes place. I intentionally emphasize this understanding of justice as a "state of affairs" in this book, and I will contrast it to other more "procedural" approaches.[7] Procedural approaches to justice limit discussions of rights to the *conditions* under which individuals can make free choices. In these theories, if the conditions under which choices are made are freely chosen by all, then the actual *outcomes* are not relevant to further questions of justice.[8] Though procedural justice is important, I will propose a model of distributive justice that has as its goal the actual establishment of just conditions. Such a view of justice can be traced back to Cicero and Augustine, among others. As David Hollenbach notes, "According to Cicero's definition, there could be no republic in the absence of public 'agreement with respect to justice and partnership for the common good.'"[9] For Cicero and Augustine, the actual outcome of the benefits and burdens of society are of concern, not just the procedures. This classical definition of justice realizes that bonds of family, community, ethnicity, nation, nature, and even love tie societies and their goods together.[10] There is more to justice than an individual's free choice, even if that choice is made within the bounds of the procedural rules. In this book I will advocate a theory of justice that follows these classical representatives, recognizing our common human nature, and seeking to promote an actual state of affairs in which the distribution of burdens and benefits is just.

Today, when we speak of justice, we use terms such as "rights" or "claims"; and when we do so, a strong Western intellectual tradi-

7. Most famously that of Robert Nozick, *Anarchy, State and Utopia* (Oxford: Oxford University Press, 1974), in which he argues that property rights are principal, and exchange is fair if it permits individuals to freely follow procedures.

8. See Jeremy Waldron, *Theories of Rights* (Oxford: Oxford University Press, 1984), especially the Introduction.

9. David Hollenbach, S.J., *The Common Good and Christian Ethics* (Cambridge, UK: Cambridge University Press, 2002), p. 122.

10. Augustine's definition of a republic is this: "A people is an assemblage of reasonable beings bound together by a common agreement as to the objects of their love." Augustine, *The City of God* II, 21, cited in Hollenbach, p. 127.

tion comes to the fore. Theories of distributive justice based on the rights of the individual developed specifically in western Europe, beginning in the seventeenth century with Hugo Grotius (1583-1656), Samuel Pufendorf (1632-1694), and John Locke (1632-1704). Locke argued that the social order could be maintained via contracts among free and rational beings. Like others at the time of the Enlightenment, he assumed that we know what is right by way of reason. For Locke, rights derived from natural laws: they were thus called "natural rights." He assumed that any person could know what these natural rights were if that person used his reason properly.[11] An example of such an understanding of natural rights is found in the U.S. Declaration of Independence, which declares, "We hold these truths to be self-evident." The rights that follow are thought to be self-evident conclusions that anyone might reasonably derive from the natural order of things. While this discussion of distributive justice will not require that we trace the history of human rights or defend it, it will require that I spell out how "rights" will be understood throughout this book.

Contemporary political philosopher Joel Feinberg has done much to clarify the contemporary discussion concerning rights. Feinberg begins by establishing a distinction between rights and claims: "There is an etymological connection between claim and clamor. Needs clamor. Perhaps even if the claim is not a direct claim against someone, it is a legitimate moral claim, e.g., the starving child who has no one nearby with food."[12] A claim, for Feinberg, is a cry that calls out for an open hearing about its legitimacy. A claim may not be officially recognized in law or custom, but the claimant argues that he has a case to make. A claim is not yet a right, nor does a claim yet call forth a duty on someone else's part. For example, I may claim that I deserve a cold beer after a hard day's work in the summer, but it is not anyone's duty to provide me with that drink un-

11. "John Locke," in *On Moral Business*, Max Stackhouse, Dennis McCann, and Shirley Roels, eds. (Grand Rapids: Eerdmans, 1995), p. 202.

12. Joel Feinberg, *Rights, Justice and the Bounds of Liberty: Essays in Social Philosophy* (Princeton, NJ: Princeton University Press, 1980), p. 140.

til it is acknowledged as a right. A claimant may assert legitimacy for a claim, but that claim may or may not be validated as a right.

Claims can be validated morally and/or legally. They are validated morally when shown to derive from an accepted moral principle. For example, my child claims the right to some of my time and affection. There is an implicit appeal here to a generally accepted moral principle that parents ought to care for their children. The unique relationship between parents and children serves as the ground for the claim by my child. Other people's children cannot make this claim on me. The claim by my children, however, results in a responsibility placed on me to fulfill my parental duty. This responsibility is not a legal right; it is a moral one. No political authority will compel me to fulfill this particular duty. In this book I will refer to such claims, justified by a moral principle, as "moral rights." A legal right also originates as a claim, a claim that is heard in a public forum. An appropriate legal body (be it the Supreme Court or a tribal council) then validates it. When validated, it achieves the status of law and becomes a legal right. If I have a legal right, I may claim it over against some person, group of people, or institution. If I have a moral right, I may claim it; but I cannot expect the law of the state to enforce it. If I have a legal right, it may be possible for me to insist on the enforcement of the law — even though it is not moral. For example, if, under apartheid, I had the right to exclude you from moving into my neighborhood because you were black, I might call the police to enforce that right, even though it would be morally reprehensible to do so.

A moral right tends to place broad responsibilities on others, whereas legal rights will more likely imply specific duties. Feinberg distinguishes between responsibilities and duties in this way:

> A responsibility, like a duty, is both a burden and a liability; but unlike a duty carries considerable discretion (sometimes called 'authority') along with it. A goal is assigned and the means of achieving it are left to the independent judgment of the responsible party. . . . 'That a man tried his best' is more

likely to be accepted as an excuse for failure to perform one's duty than for failure to fulfill one's responsibility.[13]

Duties are specific responses to the demands brought about by particular rights, whereas responsibilities may be laid on persons without specific demands. For example, I have the responsibility to be a good parent to my children. This responsibility may entail a nearly endless set of duties. Unlike rights, responsibilities are not commanded and may be executed in a number of possible ways. A duty, on the other hand, requires obedience to a specific command. Here is a biblical example that will arise in the course of my argument: the people of Israel were *responsible* to care for the widows, orphans, and aliens in their society. They were *commanded* to fulfill specific *duties* inscribed in *law* codes — such as leaving gleanings in the field, giving alms, and so forth — in order to meet this *responsibility*. Thus there are connections among the terms here, and I will discuss this relationship between ancient moral standards and contemporary rights at greater length later.

For a right to be effective, a person must both have, and *know* that she or he has, that right. If a person does not know she has a right, she may not claim that right. If, for example, I have a right to a low-interest loan for first-time homebuyers but am unaware of it, I will not claim it. At the same time, having a right does not require that a person will always claim it. For example, I could have the right to play tennis at my club but never claim that right by reserving a court in my name. To have a right means both to know what one is due and to know how one might make the claim.

There are many ways to categorize the various kinds of rights and duties.[14] A common conceptualization for the various kinds of rights is: commutative, negative, and positive. Commutative rights are those that result from agreements *among* individuals. Contemporary econ-

---

13. Feinberg, p. 137.
14. See Feinberg, "Duties, Rights, and Claims," in *Rights, Justice and the Bounds of Liberty*.

omist and philosopher John Davis says: "Commutative justice concerns whether exchange is fair, such as in connection with the payment of wages and the setting of prices."[15] For example, we may agree that you will provide piano lessons for my daughter on Wednesdays for $25.00 a half hour. Once that agreement is in place, it establishes my daughter's right to receive the lesson and your right to receive the $25.00 payment. Business relies on commutative justice.

Negative rights typically include freedom *from* harms to our person or property; they have also been called "armchair rights" because they make no direct demand on any respondent. For instance, my right to hold property is maintained as long as you do not rise from your armchair to take it from me. Negative rights are frequently expressed in laws that prohibit you from acting in certain ways that harm me, or what belongs to me, and those laws may punish you when you do so.

The third category of rights in this conceptualization, positive rights, grant that someone has a right *to* something, and they are thought to require positive action on the part of a person who has a claim made against him or her. For example, in the United States all children of citizens have the right to an education up through the level of twelfth grade. Economic rights are also often seen as falling into this "positive" category. For example, Article 25 of the Universal Declaration of Human Rights, published by the United Nations in 1948, says: "Everyone has the right to a standard of living adequate for the health and well-being of himself and of his family including food, clothing, housing and medical care and necessary social services."[16] Based on the distinction between moral and legal rights made above, it seems clear that a claim to basic sustenance is one that appeals to a moral principle, but one that has not yet been ratified in law. In this conceptualization, a right to sustenance would be a positive, moral right.

15. John Davis, "Justice," in *Encyclopedia of Political Economy*, ed. Phillip Anthony O'Hara (London: Routledge, 1999), pp. 596-97.

16. Quoted in, among other places, Ian Brownlie, *Basic Documents on Human Rights* (Oxford: Clarendon Press, 1992), p. 26.

While the terms "positive" and "negative" rights are common, and easy to conceptualize, the distinction is in fact difficult to maintain. Political philosopher Henry Shue notes:

> In the case of rights to physical security, it may be possible to avoid violating someone's rights to physical security yourself by merely refraining from acting in any of the ways that would constitute violations. But it is impossible to protect anyone's rights to physical security without taking, or making payments toward the taking of, a wide range of positive actions.[17]

By positive actions Shue means matters such as paying the police and the prison guards, electing judges, maintaining courts, and so forth. In short, the negative right to physical security requires numerous positive actions. Thus, while we may speak of rights as "negative" and "positive," we recognize that they are better conceived of as on a continuum of rights — rather than as discrete kinds of rights.

These, then, are some terms I will use when speaking of justice. While recognizing that these definitions themselves can be contested, I will go forward with these initial clarifications, explicating and justifying my usage along the way. As I have indicated above, my goal is to affirm a theory of distributive justice in which the needs of people like Ester are met. The two realities shaping this argument are contemporary market economics and Christian ethics. Given my goal, and these realities, my first task will be to describe how and why benefits and burdens are actually distributed within contemporary capitalist societies.

---

17. Henry Shue, *Basic Rights: Subsistence, Affluence, and U.S. Foreign Policy* (Princeton, NJ: Princeton University Press, 1980), p. 37.

CHAPTER TWO

Using the Free Market as Distributor

*They [the rich] are led by an invisible hand to make nearly
the same distribution of the necessaries of life, which would
have been made, had the earth been divided into equal portions among all its inhabitants. . . .*

Adam Smith, *Moral Sentiments*

Adam Smith (1723-1790)

People have always exchanged goods in markets and bazaars, but
only within recent history has the market itself *directed* the distribution of goods. It is not until late in the eighteenth century that we begin to see "capitalist societies." Prior to that, political, ecclesiastical,
or familial authorities controlled distribution. Markets existed, but
only as a tool in the service of these other institutions or powers. The
market was not "free," since outside forces controlled it. For example, a king may have commanded that thousands of peacocks and
peahens be raised to promenade in his garden, or a prince might have
given his brother-in-law a monopoly on the timber trade, or the cob-
blers' guild might have declared only certain styles of shoes as legiti-

mate for manufacture. That is, commands originating from outside the market itself, rather than market demand, drove such trade. Since the last half of the eighteenth century, however, most Western nations, as well as some others, have used the market itself as the primary mechanism for distributing their goods and services. It is the description of the market as "free" of control by other powers or spheres of influence that characterizes capitalist societies. Capitalist societies certainly may restrain the market, but it is the market that is seen as the rightful and independent means for distribution of goods and services. Societies that use the market as the principal means of distribution are rightly considered "capitalist societies."[1]

In 1776, the Enlightenment philosopher Adam Smith published his classic book *An Inquiry into the Nature and Causes of the Wealth of Nations*,[2] which inaugurated free-market economics. In this chapter I will discuss Smith's seminal teachings on the free market; then I will show how mainstream economic theorists have developed these guiding principles; finally, I will describe how this economic theory shapes a conceptual framework of distributive justice.

Adam Smith sought answers to the compelling political and moral issues of his time. Chief among these issues was the quest to understand how unruly human passions might be regulated by *reason*. Smith and others believed that human passions or "enthusiasms" had to be tamed in order to prevent societal chaos. Thomas Hobbes (1588-1679), Smith's philosophical predecessor, famously addressed this problem through the theoretical creation of an all-powerful "Leviathan,"[3] a governmental power that could overcome the unruly desires of the individual by force, thus maintaining public order. While Smith agreed that political authority could control hu-

---

1. See Robert Heilbroner, *The Nature and Logic of Capitalism* (New York: W. W. Norton & Co., 1985), especially chapters 1-3, for a history of the development of capitalist societies and what makes them unique.

2. Adam Smith, *An Inquiry into the Nature and Causes of the Wealth of Nations* (Oxford: Oxford University Press, Glasgow edition, 1976; reprinted by the Liberty Press, 1981). Hereafter — Smith, *Wealth*.

3. Thomas Hobbes, *Leviathan* (New York: Dutton, Everyman's Library, 1950).

man passions, he also believed that appealing to the *interests* of the individual could regulate passions; these interests he called their "utility," by which he meant the benefit that citizens derive from obeying the law and keeping the peace.[4] Instead of curbing the passions by superior force, Smith thought the power of human "enthusiasms" could be ameliorated by encouraging individuals to make choices that would benefit both themselves and others. The citizen, Smith argued, has two potential motives for reining in unruly passions: fear and gain. Superior power played on fear, but Smith believed the desire for personal gain might be as effective a tool to control the passions.

In his earlier book, *The Theory of Moral Sentiments,* Smith asked how self-interested humans might be induced to suspend their own selfish considerations and instead form rational, disinterested moral judgments.[5] This had been accomplished by the church's instructions in earlier times, but by the time of the Enlightenment, that authority was no longer widely acknowledged. Smith well recognized the inherent selfishness of human nature: "All for ourselves, and nothing for other people, seems, in every age of the world, to have been the vile maxim of the masters of mankind."[6] Nevertheless, he believed that stronger influences could rein in that greediness. Greater, he thought, even than our desire for gain is our desire for the approval of others. In order to gain the favor of others, we examine our reason and conscience to determine which actions will gain the

---

4. "There are two principles which induce men to enter into a civil society, which we shall call the principles of authority and utility." Adam Smith, *Lecture on Jurisprudence* (Oxford: Oxford University Press, Glasgow edition, 1978; reprinted by the Liberty Press, 1982), p. 401. Hereafter — Smith, *LJ.*

5. E.g.: "But the most perfect knowledge of those rules [of prudence, justice, and benevolence] will not alone enable him to act in this manner: his own passions are very apt to mislead him; sometimes to drive him and sometimes to seduce him to violate all the rules which he himself, in all his sober and cool hours, approves of." Smith, *The Theory of Moral Sentiments* (Oxford: Oxford University Press, Glasgow edition, 1976; reprinted by the Liberty Press, 1982), ch. VI, sec. III ("Of Self Command"), p. 237. Hereafter — Smith, *MS.*

6. Smith, *Wealth,* p. 418.

empathy of others. Then we perform those actions that will likely gain their favor. Smith assumed that we would rather spurn our passions than risk the disfavor of our peers. Thus the desire to win the approval of others could serve to restrain our individual passions.[7]

But if we are seeking the favor of our peers, how can we be sure which actions will lead to their approval? Smith answers that "reason" will be the proper judge: "It is reason, principle, conscience, the inhabitant of the breast, the man within, the great judge and arbiter of our conduct."[8] Reason is divinely informed and can be relied on to show us which course of action is right.[9] However, a problem arises: even if we try to act in a way that will earn the approval and empathy of others, we cannot always be sure that those actions will in fact bring about the results we anticipate. It is simply impossible to predict all the eventual consequences of our actions when we do not know how others will act in turn. What we intend for good might actually result in evil. Smith believed, however, that people who pursued their rational interests would, without their intending to do so, automatically bring about useful social outcomes via trading in the marketplace. This pleasant confluence of private, selfish interest serving the public good he attributed to the workings of the "Invisible Hand." Smith says:

> The rich only select from the heap what is most precious and agreeable. They consume little more than the poor, and in spite of their natural selfishness and rapacity, though they mean only their own conveniency, though the sole end which they propose from the labours of all the thousands whom they employ, be the gratification of their own vain and insatiable desires, they divide with the poor the produce of all their improvements. They are led by an *invisible hand* to make nearly

7. Smith, *MS*, pp. 113-14, 116-17, 126-27, 166-67, 309-10.
8. Smith, *MS*, p. 137.
9. Smith, *MS*, p. 131; see also Robert Heilbroner, *The Essential Adam Smith* (New York: W. W. Norton & Co., 1986), pp. 107-44 for Smith's understanding of the relationship between reason and deity.

the same distribution of the necessaries of life, which would have been made, had the earth been divided into equal portions among all its inhabitants, and thus without intending it, without knowing it, advance the interest of the society, and afford means to the multiplication of the species. When Providence divided the earth among a few lordly masters, it neither forgot nor abandoned the real happiness of human life; they are in no respect inferior to those who would seem so much above them.[10]

The providential "Invisible Hand," therefore, causes personal interest to serve the public good.

The economic process that would enable mutually beneficial trade to occur required a "division of labor."[11] In economies where labor is not specialized, people are condemned to inefficiency. If each person were to produce only the goods needed for himself, no one would produce any goods efficiently. However, if people begin to divide up production according to specialties, each person can profit from the expertise of the other. Smith's most famous example of the increase in productivity resulting from the division of labor was that of the pin factory.[12] He notes that one man by himself could produce but one pin per day. However, if the labor were divided so that ten men each specialized in the particular tasks of pin-making, such as pulling wire, straightening it, cutting, pointing, and so forth, they could produce nearly 48,000 pins in a day. While one man might move inefficiently from one task to the next, ten specialized workers could maintain an efficient level of ongoing production. While the dexterity of particular workmen, the proximity of related trades, and

10. Smith, *MS*, p. 184.

11. Smith begins his entire economic program with this subject. The first sentence of *The Wealth of Nations* reads: "The greatest improvement in the productive powers of labour, and the greater part of the skill, dexterity, and judgment with which it is any where directed, or applied, seem to have been the effects of the division of labour." Smith, *Wealth*, p. 13.

12. Smith, *Wealth*, pp. 14-15.

the use of machinery might all contribute to the wealth of a nation,[13] the underlying cause of the increase in wealth was the division of labor. The division of labor is made possible by the market, which allows people to specialize in certain aspects of production. In turn, their increased volume of production permits them to satisfy greater demand. The laborers themselves would then desire products made by others. Thus additional, specialized labor creates both a demand for products and a demand for additional labor, extending the market yet further.

Smith recognized, however, that not everyone might be able to labor in the marketplace or purchase goods within it. He believed that, in order to participate in the market, a person would initially need to have at least a year's supply of goods put aside for personal consumption, since he would no longer be making all the things needed for himself. He says:

> Before labour can be divided some accumulation of stock is necessary; a poor man with no stock can never begin a manufacture. Before a man can commence farming, he must at least have laid in a year's provision, because he does not receive the fruits of his labour till the end of the season.[14]

Only after accumulating these basic provisions could someone go on to produce goods for trade in the marketplace.

The division of labor would produce wealth not only for the individual, but also for the nation. In Smith's view, a nation's wealth can be understood as the total product of the nation divided by that nation's population.[15] If there were relatively few who produced and a great number who consumed, the relative wealth of the nation would be small, and vice versa. Smith viewed only those who were direct producers of goods as contributors to national wealth. He saw

13. Smith, *Wealth*, p. 17; also *LJ*, p. 345.

14. Smith, *LJ*, p. 521.

15. Later formally developed into the measure of "per capita GDP" by Simon Kuznets and others.

members of groups such as the gentry and the army as nonproducers, and he viewed even merchants in that light because they only altered or resold products after they had been manufactured.[16]

Though he recognized that the market would not distribute wealth equally, Smith assumed that, within a properly functioning market economy, the entire population would necessarily receive basic sustenance:

> There is, however, a certain rate below which it seems impossible to reduce, for any considerable time, the ordinary wages even of the lowest species of labour. A man must always live by his work, and his wages must at least be sufficient to maintain him. They must even upon most occasions be somewhat more; otherwise it would be impossible for him to bring up a family, and the race of such workmen could not last beyond the first generation.[17]

In an economy governed by the market, the lowliest laborer would thus be virtually guaranteed a living wage. The reason for this is more practical than moral. Manufacturers cannot produce goods without labor, and labor cannot survive without basic sustenance. Thus if manufacturers want to maintain their labor supply, they must provide laborers with sufficient wages to meet their basic needs.

Smith also assumed that there would be a ripple effect in the development of trade, in which the market would grow from local to national and international levels. While in Smith's time it was still possible for individuals to live off the "commons,"[18] those who chose to participate in the marketplace would provide the basic resources for use in village life. These basic resources would make it possible for smaller manufacturers to develop in towns and cities.

16. Smith, *Wealth*, pp. 330-35.
17. Smith, *Wealth*, p. 85.
18. See Carol Johnston, *The Wealth or Health of Nations* (Cleveland: The Pilgrim Press, 1998), for a history of the role of land in economic theory.

Such manufacturers could then create products efficiently for larger markets. Finally, when the industries had developed to a national level, they might go on to compete internationally, causing still greater efficiencies to occur among all the nations who participated in the market economy.[19]

Market production was always to be driven by consumer demand. For Smith, "consumption is the sole end and purpose of all production; and the interest of the producer ought to be attended to, only so far as it may be necessary for promoting that of the consumer."[20] This belief that the satisfaction of consumer demand was the sole goal of production was absent among most of Smith's contemporaries. By contrast, another school of economic theorists called "mercantilists," such as Thomas Mun and Sir James Steuart,[21] believed that a nation's wealth could be measured by their accumulation of precious metals: if a nation's treasury held great amounts of gold, they thought of it as rich. But Smith pointed out that the value of gold could increase or decline, and that its value was finally dependent on the value of the labor used to mine it. Furthermore, whereas money used in exchange could flow through an economy and satisfy consumer demand, idle gold was of little value in satisfying real human demand.[22] For Smith, the characteristic mark of increasing wealth was a growing population,[23] since this was the real proof that "the necessaries and conveniences of life" were being produced in abundance.

Smith's concern was the prosperity of the entire nation. He was what we would think of today as a philosopher, a legal theorist, and an economist all rolled into one thinker. He described the field of research he is known for founding as "political economy."

---

19. Smith, *Wealth*, pp. 31-34, 411-12.
20. Heilbroner, *The Essential Adam Smith*, p. 284.
21. See Ingrid Hahne Rima, *The Development of Economic Analysis* (London: Routledge, 1996), pp. 31-41, for a description of mercantilism.
22. Smith, *Wealth*, pp. 207-8, 256.
23. Smith, *Wealth*, pp. 87-88.

Political economy, considered as a branch of the science of a statesman or legislator, proposes two distinct objects; first, to provide a plentiful revenue or subsistence for the people, or more properly to enable them to provide such a revenue or subsistence for themselves; and secondly, to supply the state or commonwealth with a revenue sufficient for the public services. It proposes to enrich both the people and the sovereign.[24]

If the political economist succeeded, both the people and the sovereign would be enriched; and Smith's system showed how all could contribute to one another's wealth, and thus the wealth of the nation as a whole. The passions of the individual were not evils to be stifled but interests that could be channeled into mutually beneficial actions. The pursuit of wealth did not presume a conflict over limited capital but a cooperation in the creation of new capital. The market, for Smith, was a system that could provide a degree of wealth and stability that kings and princes never could.

Exchange in Europe in Smith's time, however, was not yet directed by consumer demand; it was still largely controlled by political considerations and craftsmen's guilds. These nonmarket entities determined what could be produced, and by whom. They established production goals that often contrasted with market demand. For example, in France, many years earlier, the "Privy Council" ordered that a new frame that had been developed for producing stockings be destroyed; it also banned the importation of calicoes, since both innovation and trade threatened France's established producers. Punishments that included the galley, the wheel, and hanging were all used to enforce these nonmarket rules of production.[25] For Smith, a freely operating market would bring such abuses to a well-deserved end, freeing the market to serve as its own regulator. The market would produce not what political powers dictated but what consumers demanded.

24. Smith, *Wealth*, p. 428.
25. In 1623, as reported by Robert Heilbroner in *The Worldly Philosophers* (New York: Simon & Schuster, 1969), p. 28.

Smith proposed that value could be determined by the costs of the materials and labor expended in producing a product (later to be called the "labor theory of value").[26] Smith understood that a commodity's *use* value might be quite different from its value in *exchange,* and his illustration of this concept was water: although its value is life-giving, water's worth in exchange is small if it is plentiful. Consumer demand would measure the *exchange* value of a commodity. In market-driven economies, the price mechanism would serve to register the value consumers assigned to a commodity. By heeding the price mechanism, no one would need to wonder what to produce, nor would they need any authority outside of the market to direct production. The market itself would provide the necessary information. By voluntarily exchanging money for certain goods, the consumer would indicate which goods should be produced and at what price. Manufacturers see what consumers are willing to pay, and thus they know at what price it will be possible to profitably produce the desired goods.

The labor market would also use the price mechanism. Laborers would offer their services to potential employers on the basis of highest bid. If a manufacturer did not bid high enough for laborers, he might find himself without sufficient workers for the desired level of production. Or, if a laborer was not paid well by one manufacturer, he would be free to offer his labor to another for a higher wage. While this process provided theoretical equality between laborers and owners in wage negotiations, Smith recognized that owners have a distinct advantage over laborers, inasmuch as they could likely live off their accumulated stock for months if not years, whereas laborers rarely have enough stock accumulated to live for more than a week or two without their wages.[27] Thus the need for subsistence compels

---

26. Rima, pp. 94-95.

27. "A landlord, a farmer, a master manufacturer, or merchant, though they did not employ a single workman, could generally live a year or two upon the stocks which they have already acquired. Many workmen could not subsist a week, few could subsist a month, and scarce any a year without employment. In the long-run the workman may be as necessary to his master as his master is to him; but the necessity is not so immediate." Smith, *Wealth,* p. 84.

the laborer to give in far sooner than the owner would have to. But Smith did not think that this advantage in negotiating power could last long. He believed that the "Invisible Hand" would ultimately distribute the goods of the earth among all its inhabitants, since each person needs others in a market, and since all people have the same basic necessities.[28]

As I have noted above, marketplaces have existed throughout time, but capitalist societies are a modern phenomenon. A person in medieval Europe, for example, might have purchased goods in the marketplace, but he would not necessarily have seen the item as "capital" that could be sold or reinvested. The modern capitalist, on the other hand, purchases something in order to produce something else that will in turn create opportunity for profit — or potentially endless investments. In capitalist societies (by which I mean those societies whose economy is principally directed by market forces) the process of manufacturing and capital accumulation is continuous and dynamic. Continual expansion naturally occurs, as more capital is accumulated and made available for further investment and manufacture. There is a constant metamorphosis among forms of capital and between money and capital.[29] That is, money is always in the process of begetting more capital or more money. As economic historian Robert Heilbroner puts it, "Money in itself is not capital; it is money-in-use that is capital."[30] This ongoing process makes capitalist societies distinct from ancient bazaars and markets. It is this capture and recapture of money and capital in a constant spiral of trade that characterizes the capitalist society.

Summing up Smith's understanding of the market, then, we see that he wished to replace command economies and mercantilist theories with market theory and market economies. The market would

---

28. "They [the rich] are led by an invisible hand to make nearly the same distribution of the necessaries of life, which would have been made, had the earth been divided into equal portions among all its inhabitants. . . ." Cited above from Smith, *MS*, p. 184; see also *Wealth*, pp. 181, 456.

29. Heilbroner, *The Nature and Logic of Capitalism*, p. 37.

30. Heilbroner, *The Nature and Logic of Capitalism*, p. 37.

provide a means to produce and distribute goods that would serve consumer demand. Price indicates what consumers are willing to pay and thus instructs producers what to make. The goal of a market system is not to accumulate gold but to satisfy the demand of the consumers. While serving their own interests through free exchange, people in turn serve each other via the beneficent movement of the Invisible Hand. The result would be the increase in the wealth and population of the entire nation.

The Legal Presuppositions of Capitalism

Now let us investigate the two kinds of prerequisites that Smith and others have seen as necessary for the market to operate successfully: legal and psychological. First, a market society requires protection of property. With privately held property, one can create and maintain the capital needed for exchange. One can claim ownership, sell bonds, earn interest, and so forth. Private property stands at the foundation of a capitalist society and must be protected. Protection is provided, for example, by laws prohibiting various kinds of theft, through customs regarding inheritance, contracts between buyers and sellers, and so forth. While current laws related to private property rights may seem quite normal and natural, in fact different conceptualizations of property have been prominent in different times and societies. Early hunters and herders, for example, clearly did not have a concept of "private property" as we now know it. Recall also the alleged reaction the Dutch traders received from the Indians when they wanted to buy Manhattan for a few trinkets: "But it belongs to the gods."

The issue of property rights has received considerable scholarly attention throughout the centuries. Some theoreticians have seen private property as a share of the common, others as something taken from the commons, and still others reject private property altogether.[31]

---

31. See Anthony Parel and Thomas Flanagan, *Theories of Property: Aristotle to the Present* (Waterloo, ON: Wilfred Laurier University Press, 1979).

St. Thomas Aquinas (1225-1274), one of the most influential representatives within the Christian and Western tradition, approved of private
property in his *Summa Theologica*, arguing that private ownership of
property would serve three good ends: (1) the property would be well
cared for; (2) responsibility for the property would be clear; and
(3) quarrels about its use would be avoided.[32] At the same time, Aquinas held that God has final dominion over all property, and that every
person must have access to goods that are sufficient for his or her own
provision. Later Catholic writers would advance this notion, referring
to it as "private property with a 'social mortgage.'"[33] Following the
lead of Aquinas, they, too, affirmed that private property could be legitimately held if used for the common good of society.

Enlightenment philosopher John Locke's (1632-1704) view of
property rights is also one of the most influential in the West. While
firmly opposing the arbitrary appropriation of property by tyranni-
cal rulers,[34] he proposed that property ownership rightly occurs
when a person mixes his own sweat with a parcel of earth.[35] (He proposed this, of course, at a time when there were still open frontiers in
many parts of the world.) Once an individual laid claim to a parcel
of land in this way, he would use it more productively than he would
common property, since he could increase its productivity for his
own use. This increased productivity, brought about by the sweat of
his labor, would then be available to society as a whole.

32. Thomas Aquinas, *Summa Theologica*, trans. Fathers of the English Domini-
can Province (New York: Benziger Bros., 1947-48), Book II-II, q66, a2.

33. John Paul II, *Solicitudo Rei Socialis* #42 (30 Dec. 1987): AAS 80 (1988), pp. 513-
86. John Paul II, in turn, cites the Third General Conference of the Latin American
Bishops (28 Jan. 1979): AAS 71 (1979), pp. 189-96; *"Ad limina."* (My thanks to Con-
stance Nielsen for this reference.)

34. In fact, Locke believed that "private property and contracts were prior to
government, and could thereby be thought of as by nature private matters; government should protect private contracts and property but not attempt to interfere with
them or shape them toward common ends." Robert Bellah et al., *The Good Society*
(New York: Random House, 1991), p. 70.

35. James Tully, "The Framework of Natural Rights in Locke's Analysis of Property: A Contextual Reconstruction," in Parel and Flanagan, *Theories of Property.*

Locke contrasted his view of private property with other political theorists, such as the Dutch jurist Hugo Grotius. Grotius, following the ancient Roman conception of property in which the head of the family *(pater familias)* held absolute sway over all kinds of goods and persons, proposed that claims to private property were absolute. Locke describes this position, derived from Roman law, as follows:

> This fatherly authority then, or right of fatherhood in our Author's sense is a Divine unalterable Right of sovereignty, whereby a Father or a Prince hath an Absolute, Arbitrary, Unlimited, and Unlimitable Power, over the Lives, Liberties, and Estates of his Children and Subjects; so that he may take or alienate their Estates, sell, castrate, or use their Persons as he pleases, they being all his slaves, and he Lord or Proprietor of every Thing, and his unbounded Will their Law.[36]

According to this legal conception of property rights, the only limitation on the use of property was the unbounded will of its owner. Locke rebutted this view. While he affirmed the legitimacy of privately held property, he qualified this affirmation by declaring that "the fundamental law of nature is the preservation of mankind."[37] For both Locke and St. Thomas, holding private property is most legitimate, but its acquisition and use are subject to the broader needs of humankind.

Adam Smith's own view of private property was influenced by Locke.[38] He also recognized that property laws develop in parallel to the society itself. In his *Lectures on Jurisprudence,* he says:

36. John Locke, *Two Treatises on Government*, ed. P. Laslett (Cambridge, UK: Cambridge University Press, 1970), I, 9.

37. Locke, II, 135.

38. Economist and historian Mark Blaug says: "His [Locke's] masterpiece, 'Two Treatises on Government' (1690), provided the philosophical underpinnings of the labour theory of value that was to emerge in the writings of Adam Smith and the classical economists that came after him." Blaug, *Great Economists before Keynes* (Atlantic Highlands, NJ: Humanities Press, International, 1986), p. 132. Smith's own thinking on property and its relationship to labor is also quite well developed; see Smith, *LJ*, esp. pp. 13-86, 213, 400.

The more improved any society is and the greater the length the several means of supporting the inhabitants are carried, the greater will be the number of their laws and regulations necessary to maintain justice, and prevent infringements of the right of property.[39]

For Smith, the basic property that each person possesses is his own work: "The property which every man has is his own labour, as it is the original foundation of all other property, so it is the most sacred and inviolable."[40] This sacred and inviolable property could not be justly taken from someone; it could only be purchased. The value derived from this labor then becomes the original source of capital for each individual.

Protecting private property, including the personal labor of each individual, was the duty of government. Smith famously observed that there were three and only three duties of government: (1) to protect citizens from the violence of foreign aggressors; (2) to administer justice within society; (3) to perform certain public tasks and works such as building schools, roads, bridges, and so forth.[41] All three roles of government relate to private property. First, the government must protect private property from outside aggressors; then it must enforce contracts and agreements regarding a society's properties; and finally, it must compel society to produce some public goods such as bridges, schools, and so forth. Given these limited roles for government, Smith believed that there was virtually no need for government itself until some people began to acquire wealth.[42]

Holding and protecting private property is thus foundational for Smith's system at the legal level. Capitalism therefore requires the "political rights" that protect private property and "commutative

---

39. Smith, *LJ*, p. 16.

40. Smith, *Wealth*, p. 138. Slaves were an obvious exception at that time. Smith gives considerable attention to slavery at various points in *Wealth*, esp. pp. 386-90.

41. Smith, *Wealth*, pp. 687, 723-31.

42. Smith, *Wealth*, p. 710.

justice," which guarantees the legitimacy and enforcement of property-related agreements such as contracts.

Psychological Presuppositions of Capitalism

Capitalism also assumes certain personal or psychological characteristics of the market participants that enable them to be effective participants in market exchange. The initial motive for making exchanges in the marketplace is simply the desire for self-preservation that trade makes possible. This motivation keeps not only individuals alive, but also the species of humankind as a whole. Smith did not believe that maintaining the livelihood of all persons would require an extraordinary amount of goods, as he assumed that all people could be sustained by a minimal amount of goods: "The capacity of his [the wealthy landlord's] stomach bears no proportion to the immensity of his desires, and will receive no more than that of the meanest peasant."[43] In light of this, basic sustenance for all would not, in Smith's view, be a difficult standard to meet.

Smith also noted a second motive for commerce that goes beyond the need for basic sustenance: the lure of wealth and the desire for admiration.[44] This psychological motive drives us to acquire and consume far more than mere self-preservation would require. Once subsistence is achieved, we desire more. We want to protect all that we have, and we fear for its loss. Smith believed that while we might desire luxury and convenience for the pleasures they bring, the deeper motivation for acquiring wealth is to gain the admiration of others.[45]

43. Smith, *MS*, p. 184.

44. Smith, *MS*, pp. 113-34.

45. Smith writes: "Nature, when she formed man for society, endowed him with an original desire to please, and an original aversion to offend his brethren. She taught him to feel pleasure in their favourable, and pain in their unfavourable regard. She rendered their approbation most flattering and most agreeable to him for its own sake; and their disapprobation most mortifying and most offensive." Smith, *MS*, p. 116. Economist Thorstein Veblen forcefully presented the thesis that our purchases

The rich are, quite simply, more admired than the poor; and the poor desire to be rich and admirable. Smith regretted this state of affairs:

> This disposition to admire, and almost to worship, the rich and the powerful, and to despise, or at least, to neglect persons of poor and mean condition, though necessary both to establish and to maintain the distinction of ranks and the order of society, is, at the same time, the great and most universal cause of the corruption of our moral sentiments. That wealth and greatness are often regarded with the respect and admiration which are due only to wisdom and virtue; and that the contempt, of which vice and folly are the only proper objects, is often most unjustly bestowed upon poverty and weakness, has been the complaint of moralists in all ages.[46]

For Smith, it is not the accumulation of wealth that is finally worthy of admiration, but the accumulation of wisdom and virtue. Actions derived from the motive of self-interest are not to be lauded, but those derived from beneficence. Nevertheless, Smith did note that there is a likely connection between some virtues and the accumulation of wealth: for example, temperance and industriousness could often lead to wealth; thus, whereas people might actually seek wealth in order to gain admiration, virtues such as temperance and diligence could be required to attain it.[47]

Mainstream Economics

Smith's theory of the market, called "classical" economic theory, gained adherents as well as critics in the following years. In the nine-

---

are motivated by our desire to emulate the rich in his classic work *The Theory of the Leisure Class* (New York: Modern Library, 1934).

46. Smith, *MS*, pp. 61-62.

47. Smith, *MS*, p. 63. For a development of this theme, see also Max Weber, *The Protestant Ethic and the Spirit of Capitalism*, trans. Talcott Parsons (New York: Chas. Scribner's Sons, 1958).

teenth century, "neoclassical" economists such as William Stanley Jevons and Alfred Marshall in England, as well as others in France, Austria, and Switzerland, developed Smith's classical economic theory in new ways, making at least three significant innovations on it. Their modifications were called "neoclassical economics." Today, the heir of neoclassical economics, and the dominant theory in the Western world, is called "mainstream economics" (the name I will use for contemporary market economics). Mainstream economics has developed Smith's work in three important ways: first, mainstream economists replaced the classical labor theory of value with a theory of value grounded in "subjective utility"; second, they used "marginal analysis" as the basic conceptual tool for their theorizing;[48] and finally, they adopted "Pareto optimality"[49] as the desired outcome for exchange.

As noted above, classical economic theory measures the value of a product by the costs required to produce it.[50] In contrast, the subjective utility theory of value, as proposed by mainstream theorists, assumes that the price of a product is derived from the value subjectively assigned to it by consumers. In this conceptual shift, each purchaser judges which commodity she or he will purchase, not on the basis of the costs involved in its production, but on the basis of its ability to satisfy his or her preferences — its utility. In mainstream theory, "a commodity is 'any object or, it may be action or service

48. James A. Caparaso and David P. Levine see these two developments as the most significant in neoclassical theory: Caparaso and Levine, *Theories of Political Economy* (Cambridge, UK: Cambridge University Press, 1992), p. 79. Daniel Hausman also sees these two developments as central to neoclassical economic theory: Hausman, "Introduction," *The Philosophy of Economics* (Cambridge, UK: Cambridge University Press, 1984), pp. 33-34.

49. Vilfredo Pareto (1848-1923) saw economics as a natural science, and his "optimality" is an attempt to provide mathematical clarity to the understanding of economic outcomes. See Andrea Salanti, "Vilfredo Pareto," in John B. Davis, D. Wade Hands, and Uskali Maki, *The Handbook of Economic Methodology* (Cheltenham, UK: E. Elgar, 1998), pp. 354-57.

50. Later called the "labor theory of value," it adds the costs of all inputs required in production.

which can afford pleasure or ward off pain,' while utility is 'the abstract quality whereby an object serves our purposes and becomes entitled to rank as a commodity.'"[51] In less economically precise terms, a commodity is a product or service, and utility is the scale on which we measure the value of a commodity.

By defining utility and commodities in this way, we create a circle of utility, value, and satisfaction. The perceived ability of a product to satisfy consumer preference becomes the standard that determines the price of the product.[52] And the fact that something will satisfy demand makes that something a commodity in the first place. In contrast to the labor theory of value, the price that a seller may command for a commodity could potentially have little to do with the actual costs required to produce it. In mainstream theory, the means used to establish price shifts from an objective calculation of the cost of inputs to a subjective assignment of value by the consumer. This helps explain the values given to some commodities that are not explicable in terms of the cost of their inputs alone.[53]

A second and related innovation of mainstream economic theory is the introduction of "marginal analysis." This is a conceptual tool that makes economic choices understandable on the basis of their potential contribution to another unit of profit, or benefit, at the "margin" — the margin being the last unit of value under consideration. When will the addition of another laborer contribute to profit? At what price can we produce and sell goods, and still make a profit? What level of production is required to cover fixed costs? Will one more piece of candy make me satisfied — or sick? These kinds of questions can be systematically answered for both producers and consumers using marginal analysis.

Using marginal analysis permits consumers and economists to quantify and compare very disparate economic choices. For exam-

51. Rima, *Development of Economic Analysis*, p. 250.

52. See S. Abu Turab Rizvi, "Utility," in *The Handbook of Economic Methodology*, pp. 516-24.

53. The price of diamonds was a famous early example, since their subjective value is high relative to their actual cost of production. Smith, *Wealth*, p. 45.

ple, commodities as diverse as a computer, a pool table, and a charitable contribution can be measured on the same scale: the increase in the level of satisfaction (utility) that each one provides. Though each commodity may possess very different qualities, they all become comparable on the basis of their ability to contribute to my utility. And since I can quantify all market choices with the same measure, I can also rank the desirability of each product on the basis of that measure. I can thus rank the preference of different commodities in accord with the level of satisfaction or happiness (contribution to my utility) I believe it will provide me. Today utility is considered not a cardinal measure (a specific quantity) but an ordinal one (one is ranked higher than another). Economist S. Abu Turab Rizvi clarifies this: "The meaning of utility changed in economic discourse. Now a higher utility can simply mean more preferred. Thus cardinal measurable utility was replaced by ordinal utility or, more simply, by a preference ranking."[54] In less technical terms, economists no longer claim that individuals can say how *much* more they are likely to benefit from product A than B, but know only that they rank product A as preferable to product B.

Placing all economic preferences on one scale provides a powerful conceptual tool. Its use implies that each individual's economic decisions seek the same end: the satisfaction of her preferences. All the choices presented to her in the marketplace are then diverse means to achieve that end. The qualities or nature of the products or services themselves do not matter in economic terms; all are judged according to how they contribute marginal utility to her overall happiness.

On this theory, the ranking I give to each market option is uniquely personal, because my preferences are always and only my own. Thus mainstream economists make no *substantive* or moral judgments about the purchases we make, or about our preference ranking. They only provide us with a quantitative tool that permits us to pursue the satisfaction of those preferences as efficiently as possible. For example, while an individual economist might personally

54. S. Abu Turab Rizvi, "Utility," p. 518.

judge that purchasing groceries and medicine is better than purchasing guns and cigarettes, mainstream economic theory itself does not judge which is more valuable; it simply accepts the preferences as given and permits the market to fulfill them, whatever they may be.

The important issue in mainstream theory is that the consumer find satisfaction. Each person is seen as a rational being who ranks his or her preferences and then attempts to satisfy those preferences efficiently. Economist Wade Hands describes this kind of rational action: "Rationality is solely a property of the relation between means and ends — being rational simply involves choosing the most efficient means for achieving any given end — and has nothing to do with the nature of the end itself."[55] In other words, rationality is what helps us get what we want most effectively. For mainstream economics, then, each individual's preferences are taken as a given, and each person's rationality allows the individual to satisfy his or her preferences with maximum efficiency. The individual is assumed to possess considerable if not complete self-knowledge regarding his preferences, and the marketplace comes to learn of these preferences when individuals make purchases.[56] This view of the reasonable person who chooses on the grounds of efficiency is called "Rational Choice Theory," and it has become normative in mainstream economics.[57]

Note that, unlike in Smith's scheme, it is not the increased wealth of the nation but the satisfaction of an individual's preferences that is the goal in mainstream economic theorizing. Whereas societies throughout history have had goals that focused on the well-being of the tribe, the religious community, or the *polis*, market society begins with the individual. In the view of mainstream theorists, the individual is king. Society is but the composite of its individuals, and societal standards are the composite of individual choices. Society is thus not viewed as an organism; nor is it centered on certain beliefs or customs

---

55. D. Wade Hands, *Reflection without Rules* (Cambridge, UK: Cambridge University Press, 2001), p. 236.

56. Caparaso and Levine, p. 25.

57. See Shaun Hargreaves Heap, *Understanding the Enterprise Culture: Themes in the Work of Mary Douglas* (Edinburgh: University of Edinburgh Press, 1991).

or common goals. Rather, mainstream economic theory sees society as an aggregate of individuals who grant some rights to society for their mutual protection and good. All rights originate with, and serve the desires of, the individual. This view — basing society upon the rights of the individual rather than other kinds of social structures or norms — shapes capitalist societies. Within the free market, then, the individual exercises her right to choose among all possible goods and services available within the limits of her resources and of the law.

Marginal analysis also works on the other end of the market system: in the calculation of wages. In order to determine who should receive which benefits from the market, economists use "marginal revenue product" as the applicable scale. Simply stated, this assumes that those who contribute most to the profitability of their firm will receive greater monetary reward for their input than those who contribute little. Each person is rewarded in proportion to his contribution to market productivity. This, in turn, motivates people to be more productive.

Finally, the desired outcome for market activity is called "Pareto optimality." This occurs when the people who make exchanges in the market are satisfied with those exchanges. Rima describes Pareto optimality in this way:

> Pareto optimality holds when we have a state in which there is no alternative distribution of commodities that can improve the position of anyone without making someone else worse off. Nor is there an alternative allocation of factors that can yield a larger output given the distribution of income and the supply of resources.[58]

In simpler language, Pareto optimality states that, given our current resources, we have made all the trades we currently want. This is not to say that everyone gets whatever he or she wants. Rather, Pareto optimality occurs when no more trading is desired. Nor does a Pareto optimal condition mean that all people have had their needs

58. Rima, *Development of Economic Analysis,* p. 360.

met. Pareto optimality can occur even when many people have made no market exchanges at all, since they may have nothing to trade.

By using the conceptual standard of Pareto optimality as a desired outcome, economists attempt to steer clear of moral judgments about the nature of people's preferences. A free market will satisfy preferences for hard liquor, pornography, and guns just as readily as it will satisfy preferences for bread, symphony tickets, and charitable contributions. Regardless of which preferences are actually fulfilled, when as many of them as possible are satisfied, the optimal economic conditions exists. While economists as individuals may well hold private opinions on the moral goodness of particular preferences, the moral standing of other people's preferences does not enter into economic calculations. An individual's preferences are taken as givens, and greater satisfaction of preferences is taken to be a greater good.

Even its critics recognize the inherent justice in this system, which rewards people for their productivity and seeks to satisfy the preferences of individual consumers. For example, in a book dedicated to showing the limitations of the market system, Robert Kuttner nonetheless acknowledges:

> Markets accomplish much superbly. They offer consumers broad choices; they promote and reward innovation. They bring investors together with entrepreneurs. Markets force producers to search for greater efficiency and ruthlessly purge the economy of failures. Market systems are far better than command systems at determining rough economic worth.[59]

The Free Market and Distributive Justice

As I have noted in Chapter One, the basic questions that theories of distributive justice ask are: (1) who shall receive society's benefits and

---

59. Robert Kuttner, *Everything for Sale: The Virtues and Limits of Markets* (Chicago: University of Chicago Press, 1996), p. 11.

burdens? and (2) what is the ground or principle for the distribution of those benefits and burdens? At this point we know enough to answer these questions in a general way as they apply to free-market economies.

The answer to the first question may be deceptively simple. Going back to the earlier example of children at the birthday party, the free market distributes goods to those who are invited. The invitation comes in the form of "initial endowments" that permit a person to attend the free-market exchange. Let me explain: to participate in the exchange system, one obviously must have something to trade. These exchangeable goods initially come from somewhere. Where? They come from our parents, our society, our personal and cultural histories. For people like you and me, this set of initial endowments likely includes things such as education through the twelfth grade, marketable skills, access to transportation, clean water and food, medical care and shelter, and. . . . On the other hand, Ester and others like her do not have a rich set of initial endowments. In fact, they may come to the market party with little or nothing to trade. So, in essence, they are not invited to the party in which commodities are exchanged.

These initial endowments are "givens" in economic theory. Market economics, by definition, describes and measures exchanges made within the market. In a sense, then, the activities of the 40 percent of the world's population who live on less than two dollars per day may not literally "count" in market reckoning. Only when people exchange commodities that register on the market and are measured in money will their economic actions "count." These people may well do a great deal of labor, or exchange goods in barter; but those kinds of actions are not economically measurable.[60] We can now answer our first question: Who shall receive benefits from a market system? The answer is: those who have initially received something of value or have been able to create something of value for exchange that can be measured in monetary terms.

---

60. The measure I have in mind is the Gross National Product, which measures monetary flow within a nation.

Those with something of value to exchange will want to protect their goods, and contemporary property rights enable us to do so. As Smith proposed, governments do protect the properties of those who can participate in the market. If someone takes them from me without my consent, the state will intervene, attempt to retrieve my goods, and punish the thief. Ownership involves not only a right to the benefits I might derive from a property, but also a right to exclude others from it. If I had large tracts of land or a collection of sports cars, for example, it would be quite legal for me to simply wander around my acreage or admire the cars in my garages — while keeping you and others off the land and out of the garage. I do not have to do anything with the property. I may do with it what I please. You may think that what I do with it is completely foolish. But you have no access to my property, nor can you compel me to do something with it. There is, in effect, a KEEP OUT sign around all private property.

The second question — on what grounds or principles shall we decide who receives the benefits? — requires an answer at two levels. The first level is societal, and the second is individual. Both were suggested above. A market system rewards those who contribute directly to it: the rewards, at least in theory, are proportional to the contribution. Thus, the salesperson who sells a million dollars' worth of goods will earn twice as much commission as the one who sells half-a-million. The corporate executive whose responsibilities are great will be rewarded more than the employee whose responsibilities are few. The entrepreneur who risks much can potentially reap great rewards. The late Nobel Prize winner Friedrich A. Hayek lauds this aspect of market exchange: "Free societies have always been societies in which the belief in individual responsibility has been strong. They have allowed individuals to act on their knowledge and beliefs and have treated the results achieved as *due* to them."[61]

---

61. Friedrich A. Hayek, "The Moral Element in Free Enterprise," in Mark W. Hendrickson, ed., *The Morality of Capitalism* (New York: The Foundation for Economic Education, 1996), p. 5 (my italics).

Undergirding this process of rewards is what I have earlier referred to as commutative justice — fairness in exchange. Commutative justice requires that people honor their contracts, that they sell to different buyers at the same price (other things being equal), that they pay wages to workers in relation to the work done, and so on. The market rewards its participants proportionally: in the measure that you contribute, so shall you receive.

Note, though, that only specifically market-related actions are rewarded monetarily. Good actions in other spheres of life are not directly rewarded by the market. For example, you may be a wonderful mother who sacrifices much for her children. As a result, your children may love you for all their lives and care for you in your old age. The market, however, will not reward you — now or later — for your excellent parenting. The grounds for market-based reward are specific: the market monetarily rewards those who make direct economic contributions.

Shifting to the level of the individual, I then ask: How does society decide *which* benefits an individual should reap within the market? The answer may again be deceptively simple: the individual may have whatever benefit he or she prefers. The market compels no one to purchase anything; each consumer is free to choose. Mainstream theory posits that each consumer maintains a comprehensive list of preferences, known to him or her alone. Each consumer satisfies his or her preferences with the highest degree of efficiency possible.

Behind this tremendous freedom, however, lies another obvious assumption — that the consumer has the money to satisfy her preferences. It could be the case that my preferences and Ester's are roughly the same. Nevertheless, I will satisfy far more of my preferences than she will satisfy of hers, since I can afford to. We may also have the same rational ability to know, rank, and select commodities; but only I can actually make efficient choices, since only I have the financial capability to do so. Mainstream economists, as a rule, do not ask whether the system that distributes goods in this way is just. They accept initial endowments and preferences as givens. They assume that the rational process we use to make purchase decisions is normal. They typically see their work as a "positive" or descriptive science; they leave the "normative" or moral questions up to public officials.

While I would dispute much of the moral agnosticism expressed above, I do not propose to analyze mainstream theory here. Rather, I have attempted to show that there is an inherent system of distributive justice within market economies. A free-market system does in fact answer the basic questions of distributive justice: (1) Who shall receive particular benefits or burdens from society? (2) On what grounds or principles shall benefits and burdens be distributed?

As we have seen, there are gaps in this system that still leave Ester and others like her untouched. Those without initial endowments may not be able to satisfy their preferences or even meet their basic needs. While the market does work superbly for those who have commodities to exchange and does provide proportional rewards to those who make economic contributions to it, it will not necessarily help those who are not able (in Smith's words) to set aside a "year's worth of provisions." This lack of basic provisions for all is what I will next address. I want to show that even a properly functioning market will not necessarily provide basic sustenance for Ester or the millions of others living on two dollars a day or less.

CHAPTER THREE

Why the Poor Won't Necessarily Gain from the Free Market's Distribution

"When we arrive at the Final Judgment, the first thing that God will ask is: 'How Did You Run Your Business?'"

The Talmud

In Chapter Two we saw that the free market, as understood in mainstream economics, serves as a theory and a process of distribution. Mainstream economic theory posits that the satisfaction of individual preferences via competitive interactions will improve each individual's well-being.[1] Since people who make free exchanges do so in their own interest, and producers seek to satisfy those interests as efficiently as possible, free exchange in the market will result in a greater number of interests being served. Thus, it was believed, an expansion of the market should also result in an expansion of human well-being. While I gratefully acknowledge that the market does provide basic sustenance and more for many within the marketplace, the free market does not provide basic sustenance for all. In fact, I will now argue, the market is not *designed* to provide basic sustenance for all: even when functioning prop-

---

1. Understood, as in Chapter Two, as a greater degree of satisfaction/utility.

erly, it will not respond to human claims to goods that are based on need.[2] In the language of logic, while an expanding market may sometimes be a condition that provides basic needs, it is not the necessary or sufficient condition for meeting the basic needs of all. I will also show, using concepts derived from mainstream economics, why the market system alone often fails to provide basic sustenance for all.

I propose six reasons that even an expanding system of free exchange will not *necessarily* satisfy claims to basic sustenance for people like Ester. First, the assumption that an extension of the market will lead to conditions of constantly increasing welfare is not necessarily true. Second, the strategy of rational satisfaction of an individual's ordered preferences may not result in the greatest good for all. Third, mainstream economic theory does not change initial endowments; it takes them as given. Fourth, the definition of economic good as articulated in Pareto optimality (the situation in which all desired trades have been made) does not require or imply that we will satisfy the claim of basic sustenance. Fifth, the economic concept of value, especially as seen in money measurement, does not in itself respond to claims based on the need for basic sustenance. Finally, mainstream economic theory sees the needs and preferences of different individuals as "incomparable," and therefore it is impossible to prioritize among wants and needs.

More Free Exchange Need Not Result in More Well-Being

Adam Smith envisioned widening ripples of material prosperity as the market expanded. Increasing the number of people whose labor is specialized would increase the division of labor, cause greater efficiency, and would thus result in higher levels of individual well-being. In Smith's model, production first becomes more efficient at

---

2. Cases of market failure typically include monopoly, faulty or lacking information, and so forth.

the local level, then further efficiencies occur as the market radiates outward to national and international levels.[3] As more people become active in the market, global efficiency and thus global wealth would increase. Smith's assumption was that people first meet their own basic needs, then — after laying aside a year's worth of provisions — go on to participate in increasingly larger markets.[4] However, these assumptions are no longer valid — for historical, practical, and logical reasons.

Historical Reasons

As observed by many,[5] Smith's program assumes the kind of historical development that was underway in eighteenth-century England and the United States. At that time there was still a frontier that could be cleared and homesteaded. Claiming and working new land was a possible means of providing basic sustenance for a family. Furthermore, agricultural villages were largely self-sufficient, having all the essential trades and businesses in place within each community. In Smith's time, it made sense to say that the extension of the market under such conditions would likely result in increased productivity and wealth, since resources for basic sustenance for all were potentially available via agriculture.

In modern times the nature of international trade has changed this picture. Today, international trade does not necessarily bubble up from people who have first met their own needs and then radiate outward to satisfy preferences in national and foreign markets. In fact, the market can work in reverse: the international market can use the basic resources of a region or nation first, leaving the local

---

3. Smith, *Wealth*, pp. 360, 416.

4. Smith, *Wealth*, pp. 31-36.

5. For a history of this economic critique, see Rima, e.g.: "Classical analysis was not conspicuously successful as a theory of economic development." Ingrid Hahne Rima, *Development of Economic Analysis* (London: Routledge, 1996), p. 197. For a theological critique, see Leonardo Boff, *When Theology Listens to the Poor* (San Francisco: Harper & Row, 1988).

people with little beside their own labor to offer in the marketplace. Logically, this is not difficult to understand within a capitalist system. If commodities are sold in a free market on the basis of highest bid, those with the most money will be able to offer the highest bid. Thus, for example, multinational corporations with enormous capital are able to purchase land and other resources that local individuals cannot afford. In a world economy, strong and well-financed international competitors hold a significant advantage over local individuals with little financial backing. For example, a small farmer may be compelled to sell his drought-blighted property in order to survive, whereas a buyer with capital reserves may be able to develop or hold the property until it becomes profitable. This is not to imply malice on the part of such corporations. It is simply the way the market works: bids at high prices are accepted by sellers before bids at lower prices, and thus those able to make higher bids will receive goods that lower bidders do not. Today, the power of capital is concentrated among giant corporations; it does not bubble up from small landholders, as it did in Smith's time. Although it was earlier assumed that business expansion (increase in sales or profits) by corporations of various sizes would cause growth in employment, recent years have shown that, in fact, "job shedding" often goes hand in hand with growth.

While some may further argue that the ownership of these basic commodities by multinationals will lead to development that enhances productivity in the countries of origin, this is not always the case. For example, Joseph Stiglitz, former chief economist at the World Bank, says:

> I have seen the dark side of globalization — how the liberalization of capital markets, by allowing speculative money to pour in and out of a country at a moment's whim, devastated East Asia; how so-called structural adjustment loans to some of the poorest countries in the world 'restructured' those countries' economies so as to eliminate jobs but did not pro-

vide the means of creating new ones, leading to widespread unemployment and cuts in basic services.[6]

Economist Ingrid Hahne Rima also describes the sometimes counter-intuitive effects of international trade:

> Contrary to expectations, international trade has not resulted in equalizing tendencies among countries between first and third worlds. Rather, trade has stimulated the production of primary products that employ mostly unskilled labor. The demand for these products is often inelastic, with the result that technological improvement in their production tends to transfer the advantages of cheapening production to the importing countries.[7]

In less technical language, Rima is saying that increases in productivity among Third World laborers do not necessarily result in an increase in their salaries, or in greater economic equality between First and Third worlds. The reason for this is that the price for basic resources does not change much, and increased efficiency in their production has the simple result of increasing the profitability for the First-World producers.

Today, therefore, Smith's system often works in reverse: the international market purchases basic resources that are then sold and developed elsewhere in the international market. The local peoples who produce the basic goods may simply supply their labor to that market at very low wages. Their labor, then, becomes but one more commodity within the international market, subject to all the vagaries of any supply-and-demand curve. The effects of this can be devastating, as Jeremy Brecher shows:

> The recent quantum leap in the ability of transnational corporations to relocate their facilities around the world in effect

6. Joseph Stiglitz, "Notes and News," *The Atlantic Monthly*, Oct. 2001, p. 36.
7. Rima, *Development of Economic Analysis*, p. 539.

makes all workers, communities and countries competitors for these corporations' favor. The consequence is a "race to the bottom" in which wages and social conditions tend to fall to the level of the most desperate.[8]

While a "race to the bottom" is not always the case, it is certain that an intense competition among international laborers exists, and that firms must pay heed. If comparably skilled labor can be bought more cheaply in China than in the United States, the corporation will lower its costs by moving to China. Since a firm has a fiduciary obligation to its stockholders to increase stock value, the firm will naturally seek the lowest-cost labor force available, since lowered costs may contribute to stockholder value and productivity. Thus laboring people may find their jobs exported to countries with lower labor costs, even though they are highly productive workers.

Practical Reasons

Another reason that free exchange need not lead to higher well-being is that some exchanges, in and of themselves, simply do not bring about good. Even though both parties may willingly accept the terms of the trade, their outcome does not actually enhance human well-being, even while satisfying the preferences of the traders. Some freely accepted trades, both legal and illegal, obviously produce more ill than good: for example, exchanging money for sex, or money for hallucinogenic drugs, or money for human organs. Exchanges such as these are often blocked by law. But even legal trades for permissible items, such as tobacco, guns, or certain extravagances, may also result in ill-fare rather than welfare.

Mainstream economists may argue that maintaining liberty requires that such trades be permitted, even if the effects are negative. For example, Milton Friedman says:

8. Jeremy Brecher, "Global Village or Global Pillage?" *The Nation* (Dec. 6, 1993), p. 685. See also his book by that title (Cambridge, MA: South End Press, 1998).

Freedom cannot be absolute. We do live in an interdependent society. Some restrictions on our freedom are necessary to avoid other, still worse, restrictions. However, we have gone far beyond that point. The urgent need today is to eliminate restrictions, not add to them.[9]

But allowing people to participate in unrestricted and destructive trades can result in high costs, payable not only by the individual trader but also by society as a whole. Some individual freedoms can entail significant social costs. For example, the cost in the United States for the medical bills resulting from those who freely choose to smoke is estimated to be $206 billion,[10] paid in large part through high health insurance premiums and taxation. This figure does not even include additional nonmonetary costs associated with the grief and pain that the related diseases cause smokers, family members, and society.

Trade need not include noxious substances to produce ill. For example, trade in skilled labor can also deprive poor countries of needed human resources. A recent *Time* magazine article described how needy nations in sub-Saharan Africa lose young physicians.

A report in 2004 found that more than 5,300 doctors who attended medical schools in sub-Saharan Africa — almost entirely at public expense — now practice in the U.S. (An additional 3,500 or so are working in Britain.) An editorial in last week's *New England Journal of Medicine* called this exodus "a silent theft from the poorest countries" and estimated that African nations pay $500 million a year to educate and train medical staff who wind up emigrating.[11]

9. *Free to Choose: A Personal Statement* (New York: Harcourt Brace Jovanovich, 1980), p. 69; see Elton Rayack's response to Friedman in *Not So Free to Choose: The Political Economy of Milton Friedman and Ronald Reagan* (New York: Praeger, 1987).

10. *Wall Street Journal*, Nov. 23, 1998, B13.

11. *Time*, Nov. 7, 2005, p. 95.

This is an example of a practical but deleterious effect of the free market at work in today's world. Market demand expressed in dollars attracts the supply of doctors, who, like all of us, would rather be paid well than poorly. Nevertheless, the world's poorest people — with the world's greatest health needs — lose.

Logical Reasons

There are also logical reasons that an increase in free trade will not necessarily result in increased welfare, especially for the poor. The logical problem of the "fallacy of composition" lies behind Smith's belief in expanding trade and well-being.

> The "composition fallacy" may be described as reasoning fallaciously from the attributes of the parts of a whole to the attributes of the whole itself. A particularly flagrant example would be to argue that since every part of a certain machine is light in weight, the "machine as a whole" is light in weight.[12]

This fallacy can also be illustrated by fan behavior at a baseball game. If I stand up at Comiskey Park to watch Paul Konerko hit a home run, I satisfy *my* preference to improve my view. But if only a few people in front of me exercise *their* preference to improve their view and also stand, my view is worse, and I am better off in the original position of sitting.

In the case of an expansion of the market, it is held that if many *individuals* freely act to satisfy their preferences in the market, the preferences of the *whole* group will necessarily also be satisfied. This argument also moves from the parts to the whole; but, in fact, the composite total of individual economic decisions will not necessarily result in good for each individual economic participant, as is the case for the baseball fan. An economic example that points up this fallacy is that of wage reductions. If my company reduces wages paid, and

12. Irving M. Copi and Carl Cohen, *Introduction to Logic* (New York: Macmillan, 1986), p. 117.

thus costs, its profits will go up. But if many other companies, or all companies, reduce wages for their employees, the purchasing power of my company's prospective buyers will go down, reducing my company's profitability as well as that of others. And it is not necessary that the wages of all employees go down to adversely affect my business; only the wages of some of my customers need go down in order for my firm to be adversely affected.

Smith's hope that an extension of the market would result in greater wealth for all its participants falls prey to this fallacy. It might be the case that wealth and welfare will be increased for *some* as the market extends its reach; but it might also be the case that welfare actually decreases for others when a large group counteracts the preferences of an individual. Whereas Smith believed that an extension of the marketplace would necessarily result in an increase in welfare for all its participants, we have shown via the composition fallacy that this will not, in fact, *necessarily* be the case.

The Strategy of Rational Satisfaction of an Individual's Preferences Will Not Necessarily Yield the Greatest Good

Another logical problem related to the claim that the process of satisfying preferences in an expanding market must cause an increase in human well-being is shown in "game theory." Game theory has been applied to many disciplines, including economics. Some games, such as "Prisoner's Dilemma" and "Battle of the Sexes," show the logical difficulties present in mainstream economic theory based on the rational satisfaction of preferences. Mainstream economics bases its predictions on the claim that individuals who seek to "rationally" satisfy their own interests will always gain. Recall that, in this view, "rationality simply involves choosing the most efficient means for achieving any given end,"[13] and that the individual always seeks to

13. Wade Hands, *Reflection without Rules* (Cambridge, UK: Cambridge University Press, 2001), p. 236.

satisfy only personal/individual preferences. But "game theory" shows that a strategy of rational/individual preference satisfaction via competition can actually bring about loss for all parties. In contrast, when individuals coordinate their activities ahead of time, they are often better off.

The "Prisoner's Dilemma" game asks us to imagine two prisoners who have committed a crime together — Harry and Sally. The district attorney privately presents each of the prisoners the same offer: if one confesses and betrays his or her partner while the partner remains silent, the confessor will go free, and the silent partner will receive the maximum penalty. If both confess and betray the other, each will receive a medium penalty. If neither confesses, the case against them is consequently weakened, and each will receive a minimal penalty.

The game has been set up with payoffs assigned for each possible outcome. If both prisoners confess, each receives a payoff of 2; if neither confesses, each receives a payoff of 3; if one confesses while the other remains silent, the confessor receives a payoff of 4 while the other receives no payoff.

PRISONER'S DILEMMA

	Sally Confesses	Sally Does Not Confess
Harry Confesses	Harry 2 / Sally 2	Harry 4 / Sally 0
Harry Does Not Confess	Harry 0 / Sally 4	Harry 3 / Sally 3

Obviously, the best outcome for Harry is to confess while Sally does not, and the best outcome for Sally is to confess while Harry does not. In each case, the worst outcome will result for the one who does not confess. On the other hand, the best outcome for both together results from cooperation in which neither confesses; and the second-best outcome results from both confessing. In this case, self-interested competition is the worst strategy.[14]

This game shows how the exercise of "rationality" can be self-defeating in one instance. By extension, it also shows how the pursuit of individual preferences may serve as bad policy in the long term. Imagine that the game of Prisoner's Dilemma has been extended to include 100 moves. If both cooperate — that is, if neither confesses — for all 100 moves, the outcome for both will total 600 points; but if both always pursue their own interest at the expense of the other — confessing and betraying the other — the total maximum utility will be 400. "Rationality," however, requires that the players do not cooperate but operate as autonomous self-satisfiers. The first 99 moves include the possibility of a payback on the following move: if I seek my own interest at your expense on any of these moves, you can retaliate on the following move. But the 100th move leaves no opportunity for payback: the game is over. Thus "rational" individuals who know that the 100th move is unprotected will always pursue their own interest on that move. But each "rational" partner will know this is coming, and accordingly seek her own interest on the 99th; the other person, in turn, will see this move coming and seek his own interest on the 98th, and so on, producing a regression back to the very first move. Rational satisfaction of individual self-interests can be a vicious world!

The Free Market Takes Initial Endowments as Givens

The third major reason that the free market alone will not necessarily provide for the basic sustenance of all is that the market takes "initial endowments" as givens. By "initial endowments," economists mean all those things that people possess as a result of being born when and where they are born. In the economically developed

14. Daniel M. Hausman and Michael S. McPherson, *Economic Analysis and Moral Philosophy* (Cambridge, UK: Cambridge University Press, 1996), pp. 182-84.

West, for example, a typical endowment for most people includes ample food, education through the twelfth grade, basic health services, opportunities for productive work, and so on. This initial endowment may be still greater for those whose families own businesses or other forms of wealth, enjoy influential social contacts, or live in highly supportive communities. Contrast the above with the initial endowments that most children have in the Southern Hemisphere or in undeveloped nations in other parts of the world. There food and water may be inadequate for healthy physical development; few or no health services are available; and productive work or arable land to till is unavailable.[15] Girls may be denied education, and particular racial or ethnic groups may be seen as inferior or undeserving. In specific communities, legal rights and economic opportunities may be based on gender, caste, race, or religion.

Throughout much of history, land has been the basic resource that has enabled people to escape abject poverty. Arable land, plus the labor one adds to it, has been the key to survival. Only within the last generation or so of human history has it been impossible to find land to homestead.[16] People today, therefore, do not have the option of going across an ocean to a distant frontier to claim and work a new parcel. Instead, people must find other means of supporting themselves and their families. Today we recognize that education, especially among women, is a primary factor that permits the creation of wealth.[17] Through education people can learn skills that make them employable. They can also develop contacts with others who have businesses. But for many people in undeveloped nations, neither land nor education is available.

In and of itself, the market system is not equipped to change these initial endowments. Instead, it takes them as given, and those

15. See the *Human Development Report*, International Bank, Washington, D.C. (2005) for data on basic living conditions throughout the world.

16. I believe that one could homestead in Alaska until the 1980s.

17. On this issue, see Pamela K. Brubaker, "Economic Justice for Whom? Women Enter the Dialogue," in Michael Zweig, ed., *Religion and Economic Justice* (Philadelphia: Temple University Press, 1991), pp. 95-127.

who enter the market with little or nothing to exchange are simply not active market participants. Their actions cause no discernible effect on standard market measures. From a purely economic perspective, such people simply don't count. The market does not change basic conditions such as inheritance, fertility of land, availability of education, and so forth. Rather, it accepts these initial endowments and then serves to distribute them efficiently through exchange. No less a market advocate than Bill Gates is quoted by the *New York Times* on this issue:

> Mr. Gates said today of the 10 million children who die each year from diseases: "Market-based capitalism works well for the developed world, but our human values and compassion are needed to save these children. Markets alone won't do this."[18]

Even Markets Functioning in a Pareto Optimal Manner Will Not Necessarily Provide Basic Sustenance

Related to the problem of initial endowments is the issue of the desired outcome for distribution. Recall that well-functioning markets are judged by a standard of Pareto optimality.

> Pareto optimality is a state in which there is no alternative distribution of commodities that can improve the position of anyone without making someone else worse off. Nor is there an alternative allocation of factors that can yield a larger output *given the distribution of income and the supply of resources.*[19]

But notice the important qualifier in the clause "*given* the distribution of income and the supply of resources." This qualifier essen-

18. *New York Times*, May 10, 2002, A3.
19. Rima, *Development of Economic Analysis*, p. 360 (italics in original).

tially makes the free market impervious to claims based on need. If initial endowments do not include sufficient goods to cover people's basic needs, they cannot go on to make exchanges in the marketplace. They simply will not be active in the market system. The market's goal is not to change initial endowments but to permit efficient exchanges among those who have fungible capital. It is thus theoretically possible to have markets functioning at Pareto optimal levels, while at the same time permitting millions to starve. Noting this, Amartya Sen describes the basic flaw of Pareto optimality used as a standard for social welfare: "If the utility of the deprived cannot be raised without cutting into the utility of the rich, the situation can be Pareto optimal but truly awful."[20]

The Economic Concept of Value Is Not Responsive to the Claim to Basic Sustenance

This brings us to the fifth, and perhaps central, reason why the free market will not necessarily provide for the basic sustenance of all: it is, very simply, that the market is not designed to value claims based on human need. Instead, the market honors claims based on effective demand, registered via the highest bid in the market; it responds to these price-based demands, not to human need. The claims of the poor are based on their human needs, but they are not the *effective* demand that is recognized within the marketplace. The poor do not generally have the ability to pay the price asked by the market. They cannot participate in market activity and are thus not factors in standard market theory. "The good" for the market is to optimize efficiency in exchange.[21] Other goods, such as the provision of sustenance for all, fall outside market parameters.

Since the economic measure of value is money, it follows that the

20. Amartya Sen, "The Moral Standing of the Market," in Ellen F. Paul, Fred D. Miller, Jr., and Jeffrey Paul, eds., *Ethics & Economics* (Oxford: Basil Blackwell, 1985), p. 10.

21. As seen in conditions of equilibrium and optimality.

market will respond to money demand rather than human need. A viable market is not a group of needy people but rather a group of people with the power to purchase (effective demand). Thus, the state of Indiana, for example, with a population of 5,943,000[22] is a "better market" than the nation of Bangladesh, with a population of 127,700,000,[23] since Indiana has potential purchasing power of $161,700,000[24] (GDP), whereas Bangladesh has only $45,961,000[25] (GDP). The population of Bangladesh certainly has greater needs than does the population of Indiana, but the market does not respond to such need; it responds to the ability to pay. The task of the marketer is to satisfy the demand of the market, not the needs of the people.

The Incomparability of Needs and Preferences

Mainstream economic theory also has difficulties calculating the relationship between one person's satisfaction and another's. This problem of valuation results from the fact that all preferences and their satisfactions are seen as purely personal; therefore, it is difficult to use any standard measure to make comparisons among different persons. Economists refer to this as the problem of "interpersonal utility comparisons."[26] In brief, the inability to make interpersonal utility comparisons derives from the belief that none of us can know or measure the satisfaction of another person. For example, I may take great satisfaction in an ice cream cone on a warm day, but is your satisfaction measurably equal? Most mainstream theorists claim that that question cannot be answered.

22. U.S. Census Bureau, *Statistical Abstracts of the United States 2000* (Washington, DC), p. 23. The population figure is for 1999.

23. *World Development Indicator 2000*, p. 44 (1999 population).

24. U.S. Bureau of Economic Analysis, *Survey of Current Business*, June 2000, p. 454.

25. *World Development Indicator*, p. 198.

26. Mark A. Lutz, *Economics for the Common Good* (London: Routledge, 1999), pp. 112-26.

Neoclassical economist Lionel Robbins, for example, claims that while we might assume that people get basically the same satisfaction from the same things, there is nonetheless no way of determining whether another person's satisfaction is *measurably* equal to my own. While we might intuit that it would be, there is no scientific standard for comparing the satisfaction of utilities among different peoples. In support of this position, Robbins tells of a Brahmin in India who claimed that he was ten times more capable of happiness than someone from the "untouchable" class. Though Robbins was not sympathetic to the Brahmin, he believed that, at an empirical level, the Brahmin's position could not be shown to be false.[27] Thus Robbins and mainstream followers argue that satisfaction, like the tastes that lie behind them, is purely personal and hence not comparable.

This agnosticism regarding the satisfaction of others takes on practical consequences. For example, the market does not distinguish between the relative importance of an additional dollar of income for a poor woman and an additional dollar of income for a millionaire, since there is no way to compare the satisfaction they receive from that additional dollar. Though it seems obvious that the value of an additional dollar of income to the poor is greater than the value of an additional dollar of income to the rich, mainstream economic theory sees only the increase of one dollar in both cases.

Conclusion

I have sought to provide six reasons why the free market itself will not provide for the basic sustenance of all. First, contrary to Smith's hopes, an expansion of the market may result in increased efficiency, but this will not necessarily result in greater welfare. Second, the strategy of rational satisfaction of ordered preferences will not necessarily result in the greatest good. Third, since the market takes initial endowments as a given, those with little or nothing are left out of the

27. Recounted by Lutz, p. 114.

sphere of market activity. Fourth, Pareto optimality equates current preferences with the good, excludes other kinds of goods, and permits destructive trades. Fifth, the economic concept of value is not responsive to claims based on need but only responsive to effective demand. Finally, the belief that we cannot make judgments about the satisfaction or needs of others is stultifying. As a result, I conclude that, as it is conceptualized in mainstream theory, the market will not necessarily respond to the moral claim that all persons merit basic sustenance.

One possible solution that is often proposed is charitable giving. But while philanthropy does perform a great deal of good, it is not inherently a market solution; that is, charity is not a required component of a market but rather an option some may sometimes choose. Chicago School economist James Buchanan addresses that in this way: "The ethics of capitalism suggest that the market earnings of resources become the property of the nominal owners, who may, presumably, dispose of these as they personally desire. They may, of course, elect to worry about their fellows, but in such an attitudinal framework charity is merely *another consumption good*."[28]

---

28. James B. Buchanan, "The Political Economy of Franchise," in Richard T. Selden, ed., *Capitalism and Freedom: Problems and Prospects* (Charlottesville, VA: University of Virginia Press, 1975), p. 74 (my italics).

CHAPTER FOUR

What the Bible Says
about Poverty

*The righteous care about justice for the poor, but the wicked
have no such concern.*

Proverbs 2:7

I have described how goods are distributed in modern free-market
systems, and I have demonstrated that basic needs will not necessarily be met within that system. Now I want to turn to the Bible to see
what it has to say about distributing goods and meeting needs. Specifically, I want to show that, according to Scripture, the poor have a
legitimate moral claim to their basic sustenance.[1] I will support this
claim by examining biblical themes such as Creation, the Exodus, the
distribution of the land, covenant law, the poor, and the experience
of the early church.

While it is easy to cite biblical texts that show society's responsibilities toward the poor, or laws defining how to distribute the goods
of creation, I am conscious of the hermeneutical questions that arise
when seeking moral guidance from Scripture. Of necessity, all readers of Scripture approach the texts with their personal and cultural

1. I will define basic sustenance in the following chapter.

assumptions as to its meaning and implications. I will try to avoid an approach to Scripture that simply uses a few texts to support a particular agenda.

The respected Protestant ethicist James Gustafson suggests that ethicists typically approach Scripture with the expectation of finding three things: norms, analogues, and virtues.[2] In addition to Gustafson's expectations, liberation theologians and feminists also take a self-conscious posture of advocacy on behalf of the poor and women when they approach Scripture. Attempting to unseat dominant views, these interpreters highlight biblical themes that show a preference for the poor and the marginalized and that have often been ignored in traditional theology. I would like to focus on the norms for economic justice in Scripture, while at the same time giving ear to various voices and traditions.

Biblical cosmology and anthropology set the framework for any assertions based on a Christian worldview, including those of economic justice. Understanding the nature of humankind and our role within God's cosmos will be necessary if we are to make judgments about what these texts have to say about how the goods of this world should be distributed.

Creation

In the Jewish and Christian Scriptures,[3] creation is seen as a gift of God that is intended to provide sustenance for all his creatures, espe-

---

2. From Allen Verhey, "The Use of Scripture in Ethics," in Curran and McCormick, eds., *Readings in Moral Theology, No. 1: The Use of Scripture in Moral Theology* (New York: Paulist Press, 1984), pp. 213-41; for further study of the Bible and ethics, see the remainder of the Curran and McCormick volume; see also William C. Spohn, *What Are They Saying About Scripture and Ethics?* (New York: Paulist Press, 1995) and Jeffrey S. Siker, *Scripture and Ethics: Twentieth Century Portraits* (New York: Oxford University Press, 1997).

3. I will not be making distinctions between the two at this point. Later, when treating the Christian Scripture found in the New Testament, I will refer to it as such.

cially human beings. Humans are uniquely capable of deriving their sustenance from this world, since, as those created in the image and likeness of God, we have the creativity and resourcefulness to develop creation's potential. The distinctiveness of a Christian understanding of the cosmos and of humanity is brought to the fore when contrasted with the two following views, one ancient and the other modern.

The ancient Babylonian creation account, the Enuma Elish, shows little concern for the basic needs of humankind.[4] In that story an old female goddess, Tiamat, becomes annoyed by the other noisy and rambunctious young gods and goddesses and threatens to silence them forever. But the young gods find a champion in Marduk, who agrees to battle Tiamat and her forces if the other young gods will recognize him as their supreme leader. The gods do battle, and Marduk triumphs. Marduk then assigns each of the victorious gods a place in the universe, and they begin to work on their sectors. Creating, however, is difficult work — and tiresome. So the gods seek someone else to do the hard labor: they decide to create humans, who can then serve as slave laborers. To create the human slaves, the gods take blood from one of the conquered gods and mix it with the clay of the earth, forming humankind. Humans are then assigned to present offerings and sacrifices to the gods and to labor in the construction of the new creation.

This ancient Near Eastern creation story has numerous parallels with Genesis. It shows that humans are created from the gods and from the dust of the earth just as the story of Genesis relates. But rather than serving as the culmination of creation, as they are in Genesis, the humans in the Babylonian story are a dispensable afterthought, created to provide free labor for the lazy and warlike gods. Human well-being — and the sustenance required for it — is never a concern of those gods.

Within a naturalistic modern worldview, there is also no require-

---

4. From D. J. Wiseman, "Babylonia," *International Standard Bible Encyclopedia*, ed. Geoffrey Bromiley, 4 vols. (Grand Rapids: Eerdmans, 1979-88), I, p. 398 (hereafter *ISBE*).

ment that each person receive basic sustenance. In naturalism the strong prevail on the basis of their genetic superiority. In fact, a species might thrive as a whole if some of the weaker ones die off from lack. Biologist D. J. Futuyama writes:

> Future conditions cannot affect present survival. The enduring variations may increase the organisms' complexity or behavioural repertoire, or they may decrease it. They may increase the likelihood of survival through subsequent environmental changes, or they may increase the likelihood of subsequent extinction.[5]

Thus, if future conditions change in such a way that the viability of the human organism is decreased, so be it; other, more formidable organisms may take their place. In such a system, the survival of the species called humanity is not a priority; nor is its flourishing the highest of goals.

In Genesis, however, God's desire to sustain human persons is patent. God spends the first five days of creation making the world, which is then able to sustain mankind on the sixth day.[6] God separates the waters from the land and creates fish to live in the waters.

5. D. J. Futuyama, *Evolutionary Biology* (Sunderland, MA: Sinauer, 1979), p. 7. Cited in Elisabeth A. Lloyd, "Evolution: Theory of," in Edward Craig, ed., *The Routledge Encyclopedia of Philosophy* (London: Routledge, 1998).

6. I recognize that creation is valuable in its own right, apart from the sustenance it provides to humans. I also recognize that a significant question today is whether creation can sustain continued economic growth. A growing literature on ecological ethics addresses this. See, e.g., Larry Rasmussen, *Earth Community, Earth Ethics* (Maryknoll, NY: Orbis, 1998); Steve Bouma-Prediger, *For the Beauty of the Earth* (Grand Rapids: Baker, 2001); James M. Gustafson, *A Sense of the Divine: The Natural Environment from a Theocentric Perspective* (Cleveland: The Pilgrim Press, 1994); Herman E. Daly and John B. Cobb, *For the Common Good: Redirecting the Economy toward Community, the Environment, and a Sustainable Future* (Boston: Beacon Press, 1989). See also Julian L. Simon, "An Interchange with Paul Erlich," in *Population Matters* (New Brunswick: Transaction Publishers, 1990), pp. 359-80, for a famous debate on the question of the sustainability of human life under current resource usage patterns.

God creates the lights to govern day and night, and vegetation grows on the surface of the earth. God creates the heavens above, and birds populate the sky. God makes the land fertile, and animals are given life within it. Then, only after the world has been so marvelously provisioned, does humankind make its appearance. God does not then subject his human creations to servitude or demand that they survive by their own wits or face extinction. Rather, God makes a majestic grant to the new arrivals: "Throughout the earth I give you all plants that bear seed, and every tree that bears fruit with seed: they shall be to you for food" (Gen. 1:29, REB[7]). The world is glorious and valuable in its own right, and its fruitfulness serves as the means of provision for humankind.

Humans can develop and reap the produce of creation because they are re-creators. Genesis 1:26-27 describes humans as being created in the "image and likeness" of God: "Then God said, 'Let us make human beings in our image, after our likeness, to have dominion over the fish in the sea, the birds of the air, the cattle, all wild animals on land, and everything that creeps on the earth.'" God the Creator made beings who are capable of taking the basic materials provided in creation and transforming and developing them for new uses.

The Hebrew terms used in the biblical anthropology are "image" *(tselem)* and "likeness" *(demut)*. Christian interpretations of this and other *imago dei* texts have varied widely throughout the centuries.[8] Irenaeus, for example, believed that humans lost the likeness of God at the Fall, while they retained the image of God. Some early interpreters saw the "image" as the physical nature of humanity and the "likeness" as the spiritual or rational aspect.[9] Others saw the "image" as the person as created, whereas the "likeness" referred to the

---

7. *The Revised English Bible* (Oxford: Oxford University Press, 1989). All further Bible references will be to the REB unless otherwise noted.

8. For a historical summary of these understandings, see David Cairns, *The Image of God in Man* (London: SCM Press, 1973).

9. Gordon J. Wenham, *Genesis 1-15* (Waco: Word, 1987), p. 29.

person as glorified.[10] We can be thankful that contemporary biblical scholarship has curbed speculation on this subject.

Today most people recognize that these terms are nearly synonymous, and the phrase "image and likeness" is a hendiadys (the expression of an idea by the use of usually two words joined by a conjunction instead of the usual combination of an independent word and its modifier).[11] Terms such as "image and likeness" do not pretend to offer a philosophical anthropology; rather, they show that among all the creatures of the earth, humans are those who are most like God. The similarities between God and humankind identified by contemporary exegetes often focus on the particular capabilities that define the essence of humanity.[12] Humans are God's representatives on the earth — and thus royalty. Gerhard von Rad puts it this way: "Just as powerful earthly kings, to indicate their claim and dominion, erect an image of themselves in the provinces of their empire, so man is placed upon earth in god's image as god's sovereign emblem."[13]

To be effective as God's representatives means that humans must be able to perform certain tasks. The texts that follow in Genesis describe the kinds of tasks these representatives will need to do as they represent God on earth. The principal task given to humankind as God's official representatives is to "rule and have dominion" over nature (Gen. 1:28). The human ability to rule is derived from the nature of the ultimate ruler and creator — God. Though some commentators see this text as implying a benevolent rule, the Hebrew terms used for "rule" and "dominion" are actually quite strong. Von Rad continues:

> He [man] is really God's representative, summoned to maintain and enforce God's claim to dominion over the earth. . . .

10. See also G. W. Bromiley, "Image of God," *ISBE*, II, pp. 803-5, for a brief historical presentation of views on the "image and likeness."

11. *Webster's Ninth New Collegiate Dictionary* (Springfield, MA: Merriam-Webster, 1983), p. 565. Gerhard von Rad says: "One will do well to split the physical from the spiritual as little as possible: the whole man is created in God's image." *Genesis* (Philadelphia: Westminster Press, 1972), p. 58.

12. Wenham, p. 32.

13. Von Rad, p. 60.

> The expressions for the exercise of this dominion are remark-
> ably strong: radha, 'tread,' 'trample' (e.g., winepress); simi-
> larly kabhash, 'stamp'.[14]

The softening of — or at least an explanation of the beneficence of
— this strong human rule awaits declaration in Genesis 2, where
God instructs his rulers to "till and keep" the earth that is now in
their charge.

Genesis 2 provides the first job description for humankind. Before assigning them their tasks, however, God makes provision for
his people. God causes moisture to nourish the plants of the earth
and provides them with a lovely garden. Then we learn that their
task is to "till" or "work" (i.e., to "keep") the place they have been
given. Tilling *(avad)* is clearly an agricultural term. They were not to
leave the world untouched but were to develop its potential in such a
way that its productivity would be unleashed for good. The use of
the world's resources and the development of the world's potential
for the maintenance of life and culture is an explicit desire of God.
Humans are asked to do more than catch the fruit that falls from the
trees; they are also asked to continue the creative work that God began. This call to develop the world's potential has been noted by
many theologians. For example, Christian ethicists Ronald Sider and
Stephen Mott say: "Just, responsible creation of wealth is one important way persons obey and honor the Creator."[15] The second term,
"keeping," is derived from the Hebrew *shamar:* it has the connota-
tion of guarding. People are to be the guardians of creation, protecting and watching over it. Both of these terms occur in later sections
of Scripture to refer to proper worship, in which the Israelites
"keep" or "guard" their holiness.[16]

---

14. Von Rad, p. 60.

15. Stephen Mott and Ronald Sider, "Economic Justice: A Biblical Paradigm," in
David P. Gushee, ed., *Toward a Just and Caring Society* (Grand Rapids: Baker, 1999),
p. 21.

16. For example, the command to keep the Sabbath day holy (Exod. 20:8) uses
this term.

Later, after the Flood narrative, God explicitly gives humans the option of providing for their nourishment by eating animal flesh:

Fear and dread of you will come on all the animals on earth, on all the birds of the air, on everything that moves on the ground and on all fish in the sea; they are made subject to you. Every creature that lives and moves will be food for you; I give them all to you, as I have given you every green plant. (Gen. 9:2-3)

God clearly intended to provide for his creatures — chief among them his image-bearers. God prepared the earth in such a way that it would grant them sustenance, and created humans with the creativity and power they would need to use the earth for their own provision. The idea that creation is given by God to provide for the needs of all humans challenges modern views that see property rights as the only means of making a legitimate claim on the world's goods. John Locke, an intellectual father of Western republics who is often credited with the development of modern rights, recognized this. He argued that the legitimacy of human claims to nature's goods must be based not only on legal rights but on each person's need. He wrote what appears to be a commentary on Genesis in the following citation from his *Two Treatises on Government:*[17]

Whether we consider natural Reason, which tells us that Men, being once born, have a right to their Preservation, and consequently to Meat and Drink, and such other things, as Nature affords for their Subsistence: Or Revelation, which gives us an account of those Grants God made of the world to Adam, and to Noah, and his Sons, it is clear, that God, as King David says . . . has given the Earth to the Children of Men, [i.e.] given it to Mankind in common.

17. John Locke, *Two Treatises on Government,* ed. Peter Laslett (Cambridge, UK: Cambridge University Press, 1970), p. 25.

Locke also says, "The fundamental law of nature is the preservation of mankind."[18] Here Locke is in lockstep with Scripture: creation is given to all of mankind for the sustenance of all God's image-bearers.

The Exodus and Distribution of Land

While they were slaves in Egypt, the people of Israel had enough to eat, but they were not free to be God's people.[19] In the book of Exodus, God claims the Israelites as his own; in order to do so, God must free them from all other powers. God's desire was to create a new people who would reflect his holy presence among them. As a result, they would be a witness to God's justice and holiness among the surrounding nations.[20] God brought his people out of Egypt and into Canaan not only with the goal of liberating them from slavery but of creating a new people who would incarnate his own holiness and justice.[21] As biblical scholar Juan Alfaro says regarding Canaan: "The land was to be a 'sacrament' of the liberation received, and the place where the ideals of the Covenant would become a theological, political, and socio-economic reality."[22]

God called Israel out of Egypt and supplied the people's daily sustenance in the desert in the form of manna and quails. When Israel entered Canaan, the people were to view the produce of that land as a gift of God. With divine leadership, the Israelite tribes destroyed fortified cities, and they routed the more technologically advanced peoples of Palestine.[23] This gift of land surpassed all the

18. Locke, p. 25.

19. See passages such as Numbers 11:18, 14:1-4, etc., where the Israelites complain that they were better off in Egypt because they had plenty of food there.

20. For example, Isa. 42:6.

21. For example, Lev. 19:2.

22. Juan Alfaro, "God Protects and Liberates the Poor — O.T.," *Concilium, Option for the Poor: Challenge to the Rich Countries* (Edinburgh: T&T Clark, 1986), p. 32. See also Alfaro, "The Land — Stewardship," *Biblical Theology Bulletin* 8 (1978): 51-61.

23. See, e.g., Deut. 9:3-4, 11:23 and Josh. 23:9-10 for depictions of the strength and

hopes that the Israelites had for it.[24] After the conquest, each tribe and clan was given an appropriate portion of the Promised Land.

> Appoint three men from each tribe, and I shall send them out to travel throughout the country. They are to make a survey of it showing the holding suitable for each tribe, and come back to me, and then it can be shared out among you in seven portions. (Josh. 18:4)

What was considered a suitable holding for each tribe? We are not told what the basis for that decision was, but we clearly see that the distribution was divinely ordained. The method of casting lots was used to show that God directly guided the allotment process (Josh. 18:6). The portions were divided by lots so that God might provide each tribe its place in the land, where they might thrive as his people.

Thus God first created his people to be his special treasure on the earth; he then provided this people with earthly treasures, such as the land of Canaan, so that they might thrive. The land of Canaan was the inheritance of the people of God. It was a "land flowing with milk and honey" (Exod. 3:8; Lev. 20:24; Num. 13:27; Deut. 6:3, etc.), a poetic depiction of a land that would provide for considerably more than basic needs. Milk was considered a luxury because it spoiled quickly in the warm climates of the ancient Near East; thus a land "flowing with milk" would imply the constant presence of lavish provisions.[25] Honey was also considered a rare treat, since finding it required very good luck or delicate cultivation.[26] Thus God's design was to provide his people with a land that was more than sufficient for their basic needs.[27]

---

evil of the Canaanites, as well as the promises the Lord made to drive out these nations on behalf of Israel.

24. See, e.g., Deut. 8:7-10.

25. See R. K. Harrison, "Milk," in *ISBE*, III, p. 335.

26. See J. A. Patch, "Honey," in *ISBE*, II, p. 749.

27. See John R. Schneider, *The Good of Affluence: Seeking God in a Culture of*

This world and its riches, however, were not to be squandered. They were to be the place in which God's people could demonstrate that the presence of the holy God was among them.[28] Instead, once people were settled in the land with houses, barns, fields, and all the blessings of a sedentary life, they came to see possession of the land as their right — rather than as God's gift. Instead of being grateful recipients of a gift, the Israelites became jealous proprietors; in effect, they banished God the giver from his own land.[29] Walter Brueggemann says:

> In such a consciousness Israel is no longer recipient of land but controller, no longer creature of grace but manager of achievement. There is no more radical word than that in Deut. 8:15: "Yahweh, your God, it is he who gives you power to get wealth."[30]

The land was not an unconditional grant; it was God's continued and conditional gift. Life with God in the land required continuous obedience to God. In his study of ethics in Deuteronomy, J. Gary Millar notes: "While the land is often presented as an unconditional gift of Yahweh (which Israel must simply accept), occupation also seems to be conditioned on the obedience of Israel (e.g., in Deut. 11:8-9)."[31] Brueggemann also notes: "Covenant law exists so that Israel will never forget who owns the land, and how it was received."[32]

Wealth (Grand Rapids: Eerdmans, 2003), for an extended treatment of this point. Schneider argues that God desires to provide his people with the "delight" that can come as a result of earthly blessings.

28. A number of Old Testament texts reflect this idea (e.g., Deut. 7:6; 10:15; Exod. 19:6; Isa. 42:6; 49:6, etc.). 1 Pet. 2:9 then picks up these themes and applies them to the new Christians: "But you are a chosen race, a royal priesthood, a dedicated nation, a people claimed by God for his own, to proclaim the glorious deeds of him who called you out of the darkness into his marvelous light."

29. Brueggemann, *The Land* (Philadelphia: Fortress, 1977), pp. 45-70.

30. Brueggemann, p. 56.

31. J. Gary Millar, *Now Choose Life: Theology and Ethics in Deuteronomy* (Grand Rapids: Eerdmans, 1998), p. 57. Millar here represents and agrees with the position of J. G. Ploger.

32. Millar, p. 61.

At the heart of Scripture's teaching on wealth, property, and poverty is the belief that the world and all things within it belong to God, and whatever portion of it we may receive is a gift of God. This belief even affected the way property transactions were executed: "No land may be sold outright, because the land is mine, and you come to it as aliens and tenants of mine" (Lev. 25:23). The land and all the wealth that derives from it remain God's, to do with as he wills. And among the commands expressing the will of God are many mandating that all his children, especially the weakest among them, have sufficient goods for their daily needs. Some members of Israel, such as orphans, widows, and aliens, were cut off or dispossessed from their inheritance. But these members of the community nevertheless merited a share of the produce of the land even if they were no longer its officially recognized owners.[33] This leads to the next issue: the covenant law Israel was called to practice in the land they had been given.

Covenant Law

The covenant was the framework for justice in Israel. Keeping covenant meant caring for people and property in God's stead, with God's own holiness and justice as the baseline. Traditional ancient Near Eastern covenants often occurred among suzerains and their vassals.[34] In these covenants/treaties, the suzerain would declare the relationship between the two parties and would set forth the conditions required of the vassal. Fidelity to these stipulations would result in blessing, and infidelity would result in curses. God's covenant with the vassal Israel included a number of provisions about property. Stipulations included the prohibition of theft, maintaining fair weights and measures, leaving gleanings for the poor, being open-

33. See Luke Timothy Johnson, *Sharing Possessions: Mandate and Symbol of Faith* (Philadelphia: Fortress, 1981), p. 91.

34. There were also covenants between relative equals, seen, e.g., in Gen. 20 between Abraham and Abimelech.

handed toward the needy, aiding the orphans and widows, and so forth.

The commandment that seems to explicitly recognize the legitimacy of personal possessions is the prohibition of theft: "Do not steal" (Exod. 20:15). Obviously, it would be impossible to steal if all property were communal. But, as John Calvin was quick to point out, the prohibition of theft also implies positive duties. About this commandment Calvin says:

> God sees the hard and inhuman laws with which the more powerful oppresses and crushes the weaker person. . . . And such injustice occurs not only in matters of money or in merchandise or land, but in the right of each one; for we defraud our neighbors of their property if we repudiate the duties by which we are obligated to them.[35]

For Calvin, guarding property also implies that we render what is due to others. This "rendering" might include such diverse things as sharing with others in need, aiding others to keep what rightfully belongs to them, or even showing appropriate honor to magistrates and ministers.[36]

Many laws within the covenant code show special concern for those who experienced the greatest need — the widow, the orphan, and the alien. In Old Testament literature the widow, orphan, and alien are a veritable trinity of neediness, and a number of covenant laws were especially enacted to provide for them. If covenant law were fulfilled in the land, its result would be an absence of poverty. Deuteronomy 15:4-5 reads:

> There will never be any poor among you if only you obey the LORD your God by carefully keeping these commandments

35. John Calvin, *Institutes of the Christian Religion*, trans. Ford Lewis Battles, ed. John T. McNeill (Philadelphia: Westminster Press, 1960), II, 8, p. 409.
36. Calvin, p. 410.

which I lay upon you this day; for the LORD your God will bless you with great prosperity in the land which he is giving you to occupy as your holding (see also Deut. 14:29; 16:11, 14; 26:12, 13).

God mandated that his people serve the neediest among them by keeping laws that were specifically enacted to sustain them. This mandate to provide for the needs of the poor is seen in the covenant legislation of the Pentateuch. Among these laws are the following:[37]

1. The third-year tithe went to poor widows, orphans, and sojourners, as well as to the Levites (Deut. 14:28-29).
2. Laws on gleaning that permitted the poor to harvest leftovers in fields not their own (Lev. 19:9-10, Deut. 24:19-21). The story of Ruth shows how these laws were enacted.
3. Every seventh year the fields lay fallow, and the poor were permitted to harvest the natural growth.
4. A zero-interest loan had to be available to the poor, and if the balance was not repaid by the sabbatical year, it was to be forgiven (Exod. 22:25; Lev. 25:35-38; Deut. 15:1-11). (Though God did permit interest charges, especially on foreigners,[38] poor Israelites were not to be charged interest.)
5. Israelites who had become slaves in order to repay debts were to go free in the seventh year (Lev. 25:47-53; Exod. 21:1-11; Deut. 15:12-18). And when the freed slaves left, their "master" had to provide liberally for them, including giving them cattle, grain, and wine (Deut. 15:14) so they could again earn their own way.
6. Immediate payment (Deut. 24:14f.): the poor, who needed their daily wages for their daily provisions, were to be paid daily. Related to this was the command that a man's coat could not be held as collateral overnight, since the poor man would need that coat to keep himself warm during the night (Deut. 24:12).

37. See Mott and Sider, "Economic Justice: A Biblical Paradigm," pp. 40-41.
38. Deut. 23:20.

7. Redemption by a near family member, by which a next of kin could bail out the indebted or hopeless poor, also served as a remedy for those in extreme need (again, see Ruth).

Concerning these covenant laws, New Testament scholar David Holwerda says: "These stipulations sought to provide the poor with an economic base necessary to guarantee a livelihood and personal liberty."[39] And theologian Douglas Meeks observes: "Gleaning rights are not voluntary acts of charity of the rich toward the poor; they are the poor's right to livelihood."[40]

Doing justice — keeping the covenant stipulations — would result in a blessing for Israel, including a great deal of material prosperity. For example, Leviticus 26:3-5 declares:

> If you conform to my statutes, if you observe and carry out my commandments, I shall give you rain at the proper season; the land will yield its produce and the trees of the countryside their fruit. Threshing will last till vintage, and vintage till sowing; you will eat your fill and live secure in your land.

However, failure to keep the covenant stipulations, including those directed toward the alleviation of poverty, would result in a series of curses, including some increasingly devastating property devaluations. For example, Leviticus 26:20 states: "[Y]our strength will be spent in vain; your land will not yield its produce, nor the trees in it their fruit." If the Israelites were to continue to break covenant, God says: "I shall cut short your daily bread until ten women can bake your bread in a single oven; they will dole it out by weight, and though you eat, you will not be satisfied" (Lev. 26:26). And finally, if the Israelites insisted on breaking covenant, God would banish them from the land they had been given: "I shall scatter you among the heathen, pursue you with drawn sword; your land will be desert and

---

39. David Holwerda, "The Poor," *ISBE*, III, p. 906.
40. Douglas Meeks, *God the Economist* (Philadelphia: Fortress, 1989), p. 87.

your cities heaps of rubble" (Lev. 26:33). In Israel, then, holding property was conditional: property could be kept only as long as God's tenants used it for good, as stipulated in the covenant; covenant stipulations required special care for the weakest in that society — the orphan, the widow, and the alien; and property managers who did not follow these stipulations were literally cursed.

Note, too, that these curses and punishments were national punishments. For instance, there may well have been some Israelites at the time of the exile who did keep the covenant faithfully, did use their property with integrity, did honor and nurture the poor, and did keep themselves from idols. Nevertheless, just as the blessings of the covenant were awarded to Israel as a whole, so too were covenant curses, such as famine and exile, visited on them as a whole. Covenant responsibility entailed corporate and national responsibility.

This national responsibility to keep covenant also extended across generations. The third commandment says: "I am a jealous God, punishing the children for the sins of the parents to the third and fourth generation of those who reject me. But I keep faith with thousands, those who love me and keep my commandments" (Exod. 20:5b-6). We can see an application of this in Judah at the time of the exile into Babylon. The Jews of that time chafed at this intergenerational responsibility, complaining, "Our forefathers sinned; now they are no more, and we must bear the burden of their guilt" (Lam. 5:7). Their complaint was likely justifiable.[41] The low point of covenant infidelity had occurred two generations prior to their lament, during the reign of Manasseh. Yet, as the text relates, the people of Judah were paying the price for this infidelity approximately four decades later.

Nor was the justice demanded in covenant law seen as a standard of justice that was applicable only in Israel. The just nature of God himself was the basis for God's demand of justice (cf. Neh. 9:33; Ps. 7:9; Isa. 45:21; Zeph. 3:5), so wherever God is, this standard of jus-

---

41. 2 Kings 23:24-27.

tice is also present. God's holy presence was seen most explicitly in the just laws of Israel; but these laws were also expressly established to serve as a testimony to the nature of God among Israel's neighbors. Deuteronomy thus speaks of the wide relevance of covenant law:[42]

> "I have taught you statutes and laws, as the LORD my God commanded me; see that you keep them when you go into and occupy the land. Observe them carefully, for thereby you will display your wisdom and understanding to other peoples. When they hear about all these statutes, they will say, 'What a wise and understanding people this great nation is!' What great nation has a god close at hand as the LORD our God is close to us whenever we call to him? What great nation is there whose statutes and laws are so just, as is all this code of laws which I am setting before you today?" (Deut. 4:5-8)

In light of this global applicability of covenant law, various passages in Scripture condemn not only Israel but also the surrounding nations for their greed, violence, and practices of economic injustice. For example, Amos 1:13 reads: "For crime after crime of the Ammonites I shall grant them no reprieve, because in their greed for land they ripped open the pregnant women in Gilead." This and other passages[43] show that these covenant laws were not merely local customs but precepts that were applicable worldwide, as they reflected the nature of God's own justice. This justice, I reiterate, includes God's demand that the poor, the widow, and the alien receive basic sustenance. Laws such as these continue to be valid; they now

---

42. At this point the reader might ask why a Christian theologian so focuses on Old Testament law. I have two responses: first, these are also the Christian Scriptures, and secondly, the Old Testament law provides rich details of a divine plan for a just society. Whereas the New Testament emphasizes the salvific work of Christ, the Old Testament emphasizes life as it should be lived by God's people in God's land.

43. See also Jer. 47-48, Isa. 23-24, Zech. 9:1-4, plus the earlier oracles in Amos for similar condemnations of the unjust nations.

serve to create a "biblical jurisprudential tradition," which continues to guide believers.[44]

The responsibility to care for the weak in society is maintained in the New Testament.[45] Commenting on the difference between justice in the Old and New Testaments, biblical scholar J. G. Gibbs says:

> It is remarkable, in view of greatly changed political circumstances, that this theme of God's social and economic justice was not lost within the early Church. It is not that social justice became less important to God in New Testament times, but rather that the Church was in a very different situation from that of tribal amphictyony or theocratic monarchy.[46]

Advocacy for the Poor

In speaking about the poor, I should note that, in the basic sense of those lacking physical goods, Jesus and his disciples were not necessarily among their society's poorest. The fishermen from Galilee who served as Jesus' disciples were small business owners. Jesus and his disciples also gave alms rather than receiving them.[47]

While the term "poor" does take on wider connotations,[48] a

44. "Biblical jurisprudential tradition" is Daniel Maguire's phrase, used in discussions with the author. In the next chapter I will propose a means by which we can appropriate these laws today.

45. Though, already by the time the New Testament was written, not all of the specific duties of Old Testament civil law were maintained. For example, Jesus proclaims the liberation of Jubilee (Luke 4:19) but does not call for the return of all tribal lands to the heirs of their original owners.

46. J. G. Gibbs, "Just," *ISBE*, II, p. 1167. Gibbs mentions passages such as Col. 4:1 — "Masters, treat your slaves justly" — as well as Jesus' comments on tithing in Matt. 23:23, Luke's emphasis on the poor, and the Gospels' apocalyptic writings on justice (Matt. 24–25; Mark 13; Luke 21:8-36) as showing that the cry for justice found in the Old Testament is maintained in the New.

47. See Luke Timothy Johnson, *Sharing Possessions,* p. 70; see also Schneider, *The Good of Affluence.*

48. In Hebrew the terms *anawim* — poor, humble, oppressed; *dal* — weak, poor;

baseline understanding of the term certainly implies that the poor are people who suffer physical want. Justice in Israel required advocacy for such people. If, for example, a king would be a worthy representative of God himself, he had to stand up for the poor (e.g., Ps. 72; Prov. 29:14). For example, Jeremiah presents Josiah as a good king because he defended the poor (Jer. 22:16). David, the model for Israel's later kings, responds to Nathan's story of a rich man who robs the poor man of his only sheep with absolute fury, condemning the culprit to death (before Nathan turns the tables on David himself).[49] In the wisdom literature we hear that God "deals out justice to the oppressed. The LORD feeds the hungry and sets the prisoner free" (Ps. 146:7); furthermore, "the righteous care about justice for the poor, but the wicked have no such concern" (Prov. 29:7).

Note that the claims made by the poor work in both directions. That is, on the one hand, God hears the cries of the poor and considers them to be legitimate claims.[50] On the other hand, God turns to the people of Israel and mandates that they be the means by which provision is made. There is a cycle of care and responsibility: God cares for the poor and hears their cry, and God establishes laws that require Israel to help the poorest and weakest. In effect, care for the poor serves as a leading indicator of justice in Israel.

The call to be an advocate for the poor, therefore, is based on God's own special concern for them. Mott and Sider see this special concern reflected in Scripture in four ways:

---

rash — poor, needy; *ebyon* — in want, needy; and *misken* — dependent, socially inferior. All of these words treat various aspects of a similar concept and are often used interchangeably (cf., e.g., Ps. 82:3f.). The poor were also often seen as the oppressed. In some biblical literature (e.g., Ps. 14:6-7; Isa. 3:15; 14:32) the poor are even identified as the people of God, since they are those who can turn to God alone for their vindication. In the Septuagint and the New Testament, the Greek terms used for the poor are *praus, penas, ptochos.* Outside the Psalms, *praus* is never used; instead, one finds *tapenoi* and *ptoxoi.* See David Peter Seccombe, "Possessions and the Poor in Luke-Acts," *Studien zum Neuen Testament und Seiner Umwelt* (1982), for further elaboration of the terms for "poor."

49. 2 Sam. 12:5-6.

50. See, for example, Prov. 21:13; Ps. 34:6, 17.

1. The Sovereign of history works to lift up the poor and oppressed (e.g., the Exodus).

2. Sometimes the Lord of history tears down rich and powerful people . . . because the rich sometimes get rich by oppressing the poor.

3. God identifies with the poor so strongly that caring for them is almost like helping God (Prov. 19:17).

4. God commands that his people share his special concern for the poor (e.g., Exod. 22:21-24; Deut. 15:13-15).[51]

The covenant also includes stipulations regarding tithes and offerings, some of which were used for poor relief. Craig Blomberg summarizes what these tithes were, and how they were to be used:

> The tithe in Lev. 27:30-33 mandates that a tenth of all the produce of one's land and all of one's flocks should be given to the Lord. . . . In Deut. 14:22-29, a tithe of one's produce and flocks was to be eaten at the central sanctuary. Every third year, however, the tithes would go to the local storehouses so that they could be distributed not just to the Levites but also to other poor and marginalized people: the aliens, the fatherless and the widows (Deut. 14:29). Pro-rated annually, these added up to a 23.3% tithe.[52]

Jubilee

The most thoroughgoing legislation that attempted to restore the poor to their place in Israel, however, was the Sabbatical and Jubilee laws. In the Year of Jubilee (the fiftieth year), most — but not all —

---

51. Mott and Sider, pp. 27-29.

52. Craig L. Blomberg, *Neither Poverty nor Riches: A Biblical Theology of Material Possessions* (Grand Rapids: Eerdmans, 1999), p. 46. Blomberg also cites J. G. McConville, "Law and Theology in Deuteronomy," *Journal for the Study of the Old Testament* (1984): 68-87, as he calculates the overall percentage of the Israelite tithe.

land in Israel was to revert to the heirs of those who received it in the initial distribution under Joshua.[53] Thus we see a strong restorative intent to the Jubilee command. The land that had been directly assigned by God to each tribe was to remain the possession of that tribe and clan.[54] The basic premise of the Jubilee legislation is, again, that God owns all the property and wishes to allocate it in a way that meets the needs of all his people.

The subject of the Year of Jubilee has received extensive treatment in Christian economic studies, and it is a contested field of inquiry.[55] Some, for example, question whether the Year of Jubilee was ever practiced; others ask whether it can bear any relationship to contemporary nation states or economies. In addition, hermeneutical issues abound. Recognizing the difficulties surrounding our understanding of the Year of Jubilee, Hans Ucko nevertheless concludes:

> Whether it is a dream of hope or a utopia that is nowhere, the jubilee is a resolve against a status quo of continued oppression and exploitation of people and creation. . . . There must be a temporary suspension or reprieve, a change of mind and conditions.[56]

---

53. A house sold within a walled city, for example, is not redeemable by its original owner more than one year after the sale (Lev. 25:29-21).

54. The story of Naboth's vineyard in 1 Kings 21:1-19 shows how this notion that land is an inherited gift from God conflicted with King Ahab's view, which was that property is a commodity.

55. Hans Ucko is the editor of a recent analysis of the Year of Jubilee that is written by both Jews and Christians: *The Jubilee Challenge: Utopia or Possibility?* (Geneva: WCC Publications, 1997). See also M. Weinfeld, "Sabbatical Year and Jubilee in the Pentateuchal Laws and Their Ancient Near Eastern Background," in T. Veijolo, ed., *The Law in the Bible and in Its Environment* (Göttingen: Vandenhoeck & Ruprecht, 1990), pp. 39-62; M. Harris, *Proclaim Jubilee: A Spirituality for the Twenty-First Century* (Louisville: Westminster/John Knox Press, 1996); and "Sabbatical Year and Jubilee," in *Encyclopedia Judaica* (1971), 14:574-86.

56. Hans Ucko, "The Jubilee as Challenge," in *The Jubilee Challenge: Utopia or Possibility?* p. 2.

The Jubilee intends to restore, seeking to bring people back into the fullness of life within Israel; it diminishes inequality; and it provides opportunity for renewed life. Enacting Jubilee was practicing true religion. Isaiah, speaking for God in a famous passage, condemns those who observed rites of worship such as fasting without also performing deeds of justice and mercy.

> Is not this the fast I require:
> to loose the fetters of injustice,
> to untie the knots of the yoke,
>   and set free those who are oppressed,
> tearing off every yoke?
> Is it not sharing your food with the hungry,
> taking the homeless poor into your house,
> clothing the naked when you meet them,
> and never evading a duty to your kinsfolk?
>
> (Isa. 58:6-7)

As this passage illustrates, covenant law did not merely require that no harm be done to the neighbor (negative justice); instead, positive, outgoing service to the poor — "sharing, taking home, clothing, never evading" — was also required for the practice of justice to be a reality.

The Poor Are Always with You

Deuteronomy 15:7-11 also shows that an "open-handed" disposition toward the poor is required: "The poor will always be with you in your land, and that is why I command you to be open-handed towards any of your countrymen there who are in poverty and need."[57] This passage is the source of Jesus' famous saying in Mark 14:7:

57. For a contemporary commentary on the theological and ethical challenges of Deuteronomy, see Millar, *Now Choose Life.*

"You have the poor among you always, and you can help them whenever you like; but you will not always have me."[58]

By citing this passage, Jesus responds to those who would condemn the woman when she anoints Jesus with expensive oil, rather than cashing in the ointment and using the money to help the poor.[59] But Jesus uses this text from Deuteronomy to expose the criticizers' insincerity. "The poor are with you always," he says in Matthew and John, leaving the remainder of the text unspoken but implied — "therefore be open-handed toward them." Jesus, Judas, and those who were condemning the woman no doubt knew the full text. They recognized that the text did not mandate that they keep the poor in poverty, but that the presence of the poor was to serve as the reason to be constantly open-handed toward them. In effect, Jesus is saying: "This woman has lavished love on me; don't you dare condemn her by your sudden and hypocritical concern for the poor. If you were really concerned for the poor, you would be serving them with open hands all the time. The poor, as well as God's command to serve them, are constantly with you." In this way, Jesus does not permit the disciples to use the concern for the poor as an excuse to condemn the woman's spontaneous and liberal gratitude. New Testament scholar R. S. Sugirtharajah notes that many biblical scholars from prosperous lands have downplayed the economic impact of Jesus' saying. But, as Sugirtharajah notes, the Jubilee context of Jesus' citation from Deuteronomy does indeed constitute a teaching on poverty:

> Jesus knew that by selling the perfume for whatever price it
> was, it was not going to solve the problem of the poor. If the
> disciples were honest about the poor, the only way to tackle it

---

58. Parallels in Matt. 26:11; John 12:8. Only Mark cites the fuller deuteronomic text. John and Matthew say only: "The poor you will have with you always, but you will not always have me."

59. In Matthew it is "the disciples"; in Mark it is "some present"; and in John it is Judas Iscariot.

was not to engage in piecemeal charitable acts but to follow the radical social redesign envisioned in Deuteronomy.[60]

From this interpretive vantage point, contemporary readers who use this text to dismiss our responsibility to the poor — "since they will always be with us anyway" — risk the same condemnation that Judas and the hypocritical disciples incurred.

Elsewhere in the New Testament, Jesus regards compassion for the needy as the standard of genuine righteousness. In the end-times tale of the sheep and the goats (Matt. 25:31-46) Jesus insists that feeding the hungry, clothing the naked, and showing hospitality to the stranger are the norms of righteousness. The parable of the Rich Man and Lazarus condemns the rich man not for a particular act of theft or fraud but for his general neglect of the poor man Lazarus (Luke 16:9-31). The parable of the Rich Fool (Luke 12:13-21) shows just how futile the constant accumulation of possessions can be. In Luke 12:33, Jesus tells all his disciples (not only the rich young man), "Sell your possessions and give to charity." In a similar vein, James insists that caring for orphans and widows constitutes true religion (James 1:27). In passages such as these we see that doing justice requires more than passively doing no harm to our neighbor. It requires, rather, that we go out of our way to do good for the neighbor, especially by seeking out the physical good of the poor neighbor.[61]

The Need to Work

One passage, however, has been used to challenge the legitimacy of the claim of basic sustenance for all. The text often cited in this regard is the Pauline admonition in 2 Thessalonians 3:10: "Already during our stay with you we laid down this rule: anyone who will not work

60. R. S. Sugirtharajah, "'For You Always Have the Poor with You': an Example of Hermeneutics of Suspicion," *Asia Journal of Theology* 4, no. 1 (1990): 105.

61. The answer to the question "who is my neighbor?" has been definitively answered in the parable of the Good Samaritan found in Luke 10:29-37.

shall not eat." Some believers in Thessalonica evidently took the imminent return of the Lord as an excuse to become idle busybodies.[62] They then seemed to expect their fellow believers to sponsor them in this idleness. Such behavior is clearly not permitted: willful sloth brought about by a misguided theology or an overanxious eschatology was not to be supported by other members of the faith community. The mark of a true fellow believer, Paul suggests, is to challenge both their bad theology and their idleness.

While this command to those with a hyperactive eschatology might provide a parameter for understanding the mandate to provide basic needs of the poor, it certainly does not overthrow it. New Testament scholar Beverly Roberts Gaventa gives us a wise caution in this regard:

> Some will be tempted to hear the command: "Anyone unwilling to work should not eat" as an inviting slogan for a new social policy. Those who wish to render this bit of proverbial wisdom into a rule of law proscribing the care of human beings for one another need to remember that this is not the only word in the canon about how people are to be fed. It is one thing to say that idle people should get back to work, but the unmistakable message of the Bible is that humankind rightly honors its creator only when it also protects all those made and loved by that same creator.[63]

As I will note in the next chapter, work is the usual means that God gives us to provide for ourselves and others. Many in today's world, however, cannot work because they are unable to or because work is unavailable. I have never personally met anyone who was so lazy he would rather starve than work. If I were to meet such a person, I

---

62. The term used to describe these people — *periergadzomenous* — may suggest more than just laziness. It seems that they were not only avoiding their own work but also interfering with others' work.

63. Beverly Roberts Gaventa, *First and Second Thessalonians* (Louisville: John Knox Press, 1998), pp. 131-32.

would assume that he had tremendous needs — beginning with psychological ones.

Shalom

Our description of the biblical mandate of basic sustenance for all in Scripture would be incomplete if we did not briefly depict its final goal. The various kinds of justice promoted in Scripture are good in and of themselves, but they also serve as means to an end — the kingdom of God made manifest.[64] Justice becomes the social manifestation of God's call to obedience. Through justice we have the foundation on which the genuine wholeness of shalom can be constructed.[65] The shalom of the kingdom is the goal. As Christian philosopher Nicholas Wolterstorff notes: "In shalom, each person enjoys justice, enjoys his or her rights. There is no shalom without justice. But shalom goes beyond justice."[66] Just distribution, for example, is not yet shalom. In the peaceable kingdom, the King makes complete peace via the Prince of Peace. And when that peace is present, we experience not merely the cessation of hostilities or war but wholeness and goodness throughout all of life. In true shalom, relationships among persons are renewed, as is the relationship between

64. Relating wealth to distributive justice and Hebrew wisdom, Raymond van Leeuwen says: "Wealth is not necessarily a sign of God's blessing. It all hangs on whether wealth stays within the boundaries carved out by righteousness and justice, whether wealth serves the kingdom of God or the kingdom of the self." Van Leeuwen, "Enjoying Creation Within Limits," in David Neff, ed., *The Midas Trap* (Wheaton: Victor Books, 1990), pp. 37-38.

65. "The noun 'shalom,' one of the most significant theological terms in Scripture, has a wide semantic range stressing various nuances of its basic meaning: totality or completeness. The nuances include fulfillment, completion, maturity, soundness, wholeness (both individual and communal), community, harmony, tranquility, security, well-being, welfare, friendship, agreement, success, and prosperity." R. F. Youngblood, "Peace," in *ISBE*, III, p. 732.

66. Wolterstorff, *Until Justice and Peace Embrace* (Grand Rapids: Eerdmans, 1983), p. 69.

God and humankind, and between humanity and the creation. Wolterstorff concludes: "To dwell in shalom is to enjoy living before God, to enjoy living in one's physical surroundings, to enjoy living with one's fellows, to enjoy life with oneself."[67] And it is justice that provides the framework on which this shalom is built.

Equality

Whereas the above biblical passages do indicate that God mandates basic provision for the poor, note that the biblical witness does not require equality, at least in the sense of completely equal goods or conditions for all. Arguments for equality are often derived from the summary passages in the book of Acts, where it is said of the early Christians, "Not one of them claimed any of his possessions as his own; everything was held in common" (Acts 4:32). But we must examine whether this really implies an equal distribution of all goods. One verse later we receive a clarification regarding the process that suggests that complete equality is not the goal: "There was never a needy person among them, because those who had property in land or houses would sell it, bring the proceeds of the sale, and lay them at the feet of the apostles, to be distributed to any who were in need" (Acts 4:34). This description shows that the motive for the redistribution was based on a desire to serve those in need, not a desire to create equality.

There are three further reasons that this narrative does not assume the equality of goods among all believers. First, the story of Ananias and Sapphira, which immediately follows, confirms that Christians were free either to hold individual property or to offer it to the church leaders (Acts 5:4). Peter's condemnation of that couple was a result, not of the fact that they kept some property for them-

---

67. Wolterstorff, p. 70. One can scarcely miss the echoes of the first question and answer of the Westminster Catechism here: "Q: What is the chief end of man? A: To serve God and enjoy Him forever."

selves, but that they lied about the property that they did give. Secondly, the verb "to sell" in the Acts 4:34 passage is in a participial form *(pipraskomenon),* which likely indicates an ongoing process rather than a one-time event.[68] Thus the passage does not suggest a "once-for-all" sale of all property by all believers but a process by which some Christian property owners sold off possessions in response to others' needs. Finally, in other parts of the New Testament, it is not demanded of all disciples that they sell their property and share all of their possessions.[69] While coming to the aid of the poor is mandated in the New Testament as well as the Old Testament, the procedure of combining goods in a common pot is not. Rather, throughout the New Testament we find a number of possible strategies for the alleviation of poverty, such as offerings, tithes, sharing meals, and so forth. Selling one's goods and placing the proceeds in a communal pot so that no one in the community will be needy was but one strategy employed by the early church to fulfill the long-standing desire of God that there "will be no poor among you" (Deut. 15:4). I conclude that communalism was not then, and need not be today, the only strategy pursued to meet the needs of the poor.

Conclusion

In this chapter we have investigated biblical teachings on economic justice, and we can conclude that Scripture provides a strong mandate supporting a claim of basic sustenance for all human beings. We have noted the special care God provides, in creation, for his image-

---

68. The participle is in the perfect, whereas a once-for-all action would more likely be indicated by an aorist.

69. Luke Timothy Johnson notes that there is always a moral and spiritual risk involved in holding on to one's possessions. "Every form of idolatry is a form of possessiveness. Whether it be beauty, material things, power, or prestige, the centering of ourselves on some created reality as ultimate involves a claim of possessing. An idolater is one who, quite literally seeks to have god in his pocket." Johnson, *Sharing Possessions,* p. 55. See also Col. 3:5, where Paul equates "ruthless greed" with "idolatry."

bearers, whose godlike qualities include their ability to creatively re-create the world in such a way that their needs are met. In the Exodus and the conquest of Canaan, we have seen that God frees his people to serve him and receive their inheritance. We have noted the risks as well as the obligations involved in landholding among covenant people. In the Law we have found that justice included special provision for the weakest in Israel — the widows, orphans, and aliens — and that this justice included both restoration and advocacy. In the Prophets we have found that God's people were called to emulate God's character, which includes doing justice, mercy, and righteousness. We have observed that these demands not only applied to all of Israelite society but were also to be seen as God's will for the nations. Jesus confirms that these laws are evidence of kingdom love; the apostle James sees care for the poor as true religion. However, we have also seen that complete equality is not mandated in Scripture, though sharing goods in a common pot may be one of the strategies employed to meet the needs of the most needy in the community.

From the above biblical investigation we can draw the following moral principle: Inasmuch as all humans are created by God and bear his image; and inasmuch as God's creation is intended to provide sustenance for all of God's image-bearers; and inasmuch as all persons are called to be re-creators within this creation — all human persons have a legitimate claim to resources that permit them to function fully in human society.

Note the many things that this principle does not entail. It does not in itself render any judgment about capitalism or socialism. It does not imply that all persons are due a "handout." It does not argue that all of the world's goods should be distributed equally. It does not condemn business and trade. What this principle does is urge that the Bible establishes at least one norm about how the goods of this world should be distributed: that they be distributed in such a way that all humans have basic sustenance.

CHAPTER FIVE

Moving from the Bible to the Present

Subsistence rights are in no way an original, new, or advanced idea. If subsistence rights seems strange, this is more than likely because Western liberalism has had a blind spot for severe economic need. Far from being new or advanced, subsistence rights are found in traditional societies that are often treated by modern societies as generally backward or primitive.

Henry Shue, *Basic Rights: Subsistence, Affluence and U.S. Foreign Policy*

In the last chapter I showed that the Bible mandates that all humans have enough resources to permit them to function fully in human society. However, the fact that this mandate derives from writings that are thousands of years old leaves us with some questions: Who are the poor today? How does covenant law relate to modern rights? Has the church continued to accept and honor this mandate? In this chapter I will build three bridges between the biblical mandate of basic sustenance for all and its possible applications to contemporary society. The first bridge connects the Bible's mandate to three or four contemporary theological traditions that affirm its current validity. The second bridge connects the terms for poverty and need found in Scripture with a contemporary economic definition of basic needs. The third bridge crosses from the language of Old Testament covenant law to the contemporary political language of rights and responsibilities used in modern republics.

Contemporary Theologies

Various Christian traditions do uphold and even revitalize the biblical mandate to provide basic sustenance for all. In this chapter I will survey four traditions that do so: two streams within Roman Catholicism — traditional and liberation; Reformed Protestantism; and other contemporary Protestant church traditions. While each of these traditions includes different emphases, all confirm that the Christian faith yet mandates basic sustenance for all. The Catholic tradition, for example, has developed what is called the "universal destiny of material goods,"[1] in which it is held that God's goods are destined for all of God's children. Liberation theologies, originating in Catholic Latin America, recognize that God did and does liberate his people, so that they may go on to serve and honor him. Modern followers of John Calvin and other sympathetic evangelical traditions see the presence of the image and likeness of God in humankind as compelling reason to provide for fellow believers, but also for all humans who share that image.

Roman Catholic

Official modern Catholic social teaching is often dated from 1891, when Pope Leo XIII addressed the difficult economic questions of his time in the encyclical entitled *Rerum Novarum*.[2] At that time the In-

---

1. The concept goes back to Thomas Aquinas, and the terms were first officially used in Pope Leo XIII's *Rerum Novarum*, 1891.

2. This official Catholic tradition had antecedents in Europe, particularly in the thought of figures such as Wilhelm E. Ketteler, archbishop of Mainz, and Cardinal Manning in England. The tradition would include documents such as *Quadragesimo anno* (1931), *Pacem in terris* (1963), *Gaudium et spes* (1965), *Populorum progressio* (1967), *Octogesima adveniens* (1971), *Laborem exercens* (1981), *Economic Justice for*

dustrial Revolution had created great wealth for a few but poverty and degrading working conditions for many, including children. Socialists responded to these problems via the European revolutions of 1848, as well as the then current writings of Karl Marx. Pope Leo, however, denied socialism's call for the abolition of private property: "Every person has by nature the right to possess property as his own" (par. 75).[3] "By nature," he goes on to say, "he is entitled to property that an irrational animal would not be entitled to" (par. 85-95). But then, turning his attention to capitalism, Leo also says that the capitalists' right to property is subject to the broader human right to basic sustenance: "Man precedes the State, and possesses, prior to the formation of any State, the right of providing for the substance of his body" (par. 115). Thus he affirms private property — but as a secondary right. The first right is the human claim to basic sustenance. Echoing this position in an encyclical celebrating the 100th anniversary of *Rerum Novarum*, Pope John Paul II says: "God gave the earth to the whole human race for the sustenance of all its members without excluding anyone."[4]

In the early part of the twentieth century, Monsignor John A. Ryan (1869-1945) took up these Leonine themes and applied them to the political and economic conditions in the United States. Ryan, too, believed that all humans must have access to the bounty of the earth:

> When we consider man's position in relation to the bounty of nature, we are led to accept three fundamental principles. The

---

All (1986), *Centesimus annus* (1991). What follows will be a very limited selection from this rich tradition, as well as from one of its ablest American proponents, Msgr. John A. Ryan. For a fuller treatment of this teaching and the reception of Catholic social teaching, see Marvin L. Krier Mich, *Catholic Social Teaching and Movements* (Mystic, CT: Twenty-Third Publications, 1998); see also Paul Misner, *Social Catholicism in Europe* (New York: Crossroad, 1991) and Charles E. Curran, *Catholic Social Teaching* (Washington, DC: Georgetown University Press, 2002).

3. This document, as well as other official Roman Catholic social documents, can be found in David J. O'Brien and Thomas A. Shannon, eds., *Catholic Social Thought: The Documentary Heritage* (Maryknoll, NY: Orbis, 1992).

4. *Centesimus annus* (1991), ch. 4, par. 31, in O'Brien and Shannon, eds., *Catholic Social Thought*, p. 462.

first may be thus stated: Since the earth was intended by God for the support of all persons, all have essentially equal claims upon it, and essentially equal rights of access to its benefits. . . . The bounty is a common gift, possession, heritage. The moral claims upon it held by these equal human persons are essentially equal. No man can vindicate for himself a superior claim on the basis of anything that he finds in himself, in nature or in the designs of nature's God.[5]

Ryan explains that a person's claim to the earth's produce is normally actualized by his or her labor. In fact, "the worker's energy or labor is the one means that God has given him to provide the essentials of reasonable life and comfort."[6] Echoing Locke, Ryan then argues that anyone who exerts labor on the earth should receive a wage for his or her labor that permits a reasonable standard of living.[7] Citing *Rerum Novarum*, Ryan rejects the economic doctrine of a "free wage," in which a wage was thought to be fair if both the parties freely agreed to it; rather:

In that document [*Rerum Novarum*] the great pontiff flatly rejected the prevailing doctrine that wages fixed by free consent were always fair and just. . . . Therefore, concluded Pope Leo, "a workman's wages ought to be sufficient to maintain him in reasonable and frugal comfort."[8]

Ryan insisted on a "living wage" rather than a "free wage." He also based the claim that all humans should have their basic needs met on the fact that they share in the image of God. Maintaining this image required not only that the mere necessities of life be met, but that each person be provided with the minimum conditions necessary to

5. Monsignor John A. Ryan, *The Church and Socialism and Other Essays* (Washington, DC: The University Press of America, 1919), pp. 64-65.
6. Ryan, p. 65.
7. Ryan, p. 64.
8. Ryan, p. 58.

develop herself or himself as a person, and to participate fully in his or her community.[9] Ryan did not accept the idea that such a basic standard of living is something that might be offered to the working-man out of charity; rather, he held that the provision of these basic needs is a matter of justice:

> Food, health, clothing, housing, recreation, insurance. . . . A living wage and reasonable comfort are not merely desirable advantages, goods which we should all like to see possessed by the working man and his family, things necessary for reasonable life, but they are required by the principles of justice; they belong to him as a right.[10]

Given the fact that all people have a God-given right of access to the earth, and that all people are divinely required to perform useful labor, Ryan believed that the businesses that controlled the earth's resources must provide employment to all those who were willing to work,[11] and that this work must be remunerated at a living wage.

> To deny this proposition [the right to a living wage] is to assert that the claims of the laborers upon the common bounty of nature are morally inferior to those of the employer, and that laborers are but instruments used for the welfare of the employer, not morally equal and independent persons.[12]

More recently, the American Catholic Bishops have produced a document on economic justice.[13] There, too, we see the theme of the "universal destiny of earthly goods." The bishops declare:

9. Ryan, pp. 59-60.
10. Ryan, p. 63.
11. Ryan, p. 66.
12. Ryan, p. 71.
13. National Conference of Catholic Bishops, *Economic Justice for All: Catholic Social Teaching and the U.S. Economy* (1986); found, among other places, in O'Brien and Shannon, *Catholic Social Thought.*

Minimum material resources are an absolute necessity for human life. If persons are to be recognized as members of the human community, then the community has an obligation to help fulfill these basic needs unless an absolute scarcity of resources makes this strictly impossible. (par. 70)

Later they observe: "Basic justice also calls for the establishment of a floor for material well-being on which all can stand. This is a duty of the whole of society, and it creates particular obligations for those with greater resources" (par. 74). And finally:

A number of human rights also concern human welfare and are of a specifically economic nature. First among these are the rights to life, food, clothing, shelter, rest, medical care and basic education. These are indispensable to the protection of human dignity. (par. 80)

Throughout the long history of Roman Catholic social teaching we find this strong position requiring the provision of basic sustenance for all. Each human being is seen as uniquely capable, and inherently deserving. As a human, every person merits access to the goods of God's created world. Labor is the normal means of accessing the goods of the world; therefore, all who are willing and able to work must be provided with work that will provide them sufficient resources to sustain life in their community. In the Catholic tradition, provision for basic needs is clearly a matter of justice.

Liberation Theology

With an official beginning at the Conference of Catholic Bishops in Medellin, Colombia, in 1967, liberation theology has developed its perspective from the side of the poor. Embedded within the Roman Catholic tradition and Latin American cultures, liberation theology takes up biblical themes such as the Exodus, the Year of Jubilee, and God's concern for widows, orphans, and aliens, and it uses them in ways that challenge both traditional theology and capitalist societies.

Liberation theology does not see itself as simply a retrieval of some important themes within theology; rather, it views itself as a genuinely new way of doing theology, one that focuses on the practice of liberation. Leonardo Boff declares:

> The originality of this new way of doing theology does not reside in the fact that it specifies oppression-and-liberation as the object of its reflection. . . . No, the uniqueness to which the theology of liberation lays claim is that of being a faith reflection originating and developing with the actual practice of liberation. Let me be very clear: liberation theology is not a reflection on the theoretical subject of liberation. It is a reflection on the concrete practice of liberation engaged in by the poor and by their allies in the field of their struggle.[14]

Liberation theology is the reflection of a community that struggles on behalf of the poor. It suffers alongside of them. Theology itself is thus not only reflection but praxis — an action that informs reflection, as much as the other way around. Liberation theologians take the broader biblical understanding of "the poor" (noted in the previous chapter) as their premise for liberating praxis. They contend that a love for and a liberation of the poor were the foundation of Jesus' own ministry. Jesus himself, they say, took up the role of liberator from oppression and of inaugurator of a new age when he began his public ministry. Citing Isaiah, Jesus took up the mantle of the prophet of Jubilee:

> The spirit of the Lord is upon me
> because he has anointed me;
> He has sent me to announce good news to the poor,
> to proclaim release for prisoners
> and recovery of sight for the blind;
> to let the broken victims go free,
> to proclaim the year of the Lord's favor. (Luke 4:18-19)

14. Leonardo Boff, *When Theology Listens to the Poor*, trans. Robert R. Barr (San Francisco: Harper & Row, 1988).

Salvation, liberation theologians properly note, does not entail merely the redemption of an individual from his or her sin; it also entails the renewal and transformation of all aspects of creation, including its social structures.[15] Gustavo Gutiérrez, for example, says: "Sin is evident in oppressive structures, in the exploitation of man by man, in the domination and slavery of peoples, races, and social classes. . . . Sin demands a radical liberation, which in turn necessarily implies a political liberation."[16] This liberation began when Jesus announced the presence of the reign of God in his own person. By proclaiming the reign of God, Jesus announced the fullness of salvation in personal, historical, and political terms.[17] In liberation theology, the kingdom of God is the pervasive reality that must change all aspects of life.

> The gospel is nothing but the proclamation of the reign of God: the full and total liberation of all creation, cosmic and human, from all its iniquities, and the integral accomplishment of God's design in the insertion of all things into his own divine life. Concretely, then, the Reign of God translates into community of life with the Father, the Son, and the Holy Spirit in a universal communion of brothers and sisters in solidarity with one another in the use of the "fruit of the earth and the work of human hands."[18]

Were the world to be transformed into the likeness of the kingdom of God, great changes would be necessary. For Boff, these modifications would include the provision of a minimal standard of living for

15. Boff writes: "By salvation we understand the human and cosmic situation totally liberated from all threat to life and fully realizing God's plan for creation." *When Theology Listens to the Poor*, p. 81. Any biblical dictionary will show that the Greek term *soter* (to save) is a term that implies a fullness of health, wholeness, and life, as well as spiritual redemption; see, e.g., W. Foerster, in Gerhard Kittel, ed., *Theological Dictionary of the New Testament*, (Grand Rapids: Eerdmans, 1985), pp. 1132-40.

16. Gustavo Gutiérrez, *A Theology of Liberation* (Maryknoll, NY: Orbis, 1973), pp. 175-76.

17. Gutiérrez, pp. 21-22, 176.

18. Boff, p. 36.

all, defense of the rights of the poor, and radical change for the church.[19] A new Exodus would entail liberation from oppression and deliverance into a realm of justice. A basic presupposition for Boff and other liberation theologians is that the God of life comes to the defense of those whose lives are most threatened, be it because of violence, poverty, or oppression. He says:

> God is a living God, a God of life and the giver of life. When someone's life is threatened, God takes that person's side to protect and promote that threatened life. A Church that defends life and helps create conditions in which life may flourish performs the liturgy that is most agreeable to God.[20]

For liberation theologian Gustavo Gutiérrez, conditions such as poverty, oppression, and injustice are never a naturally occurring or ordinary situation: "The question of poverty is a question of the very meaning of life and the collective course of humanity. Poverty is the result of a system which institutionalizes privileges for some and poverty, humiliation, and death for others."[21] These structures must be challenged, therefore, with the life-generating power of the gospel. As God came to the aid of the poor in Scripture by extending his mercy and justice to them, so too must God's people come to the aid of the poor, the exiled, and the oppressed today. The only hope of the poor is God, since they have no human status or possessions to rely on. Therefore, God comes to their aid, stands by them, and saves them; and if someone would be called a disciple of this God, he or she must also show solidarity with the poor and carry out the work of God on their behalf. Boff again:

19. Boff, p. 38.
20. Boff, p. 40.
21. Gustavo Gutiérrez, "The Violence of a System," in Jacques Pohier and Dietmar Mieth, eds., *Concilium: Christian Ethics and Economics — the North-South Conflict* (Edinburgh: T&T Clark, 1980), p. 93. See also Conference of Latin American Bishops, *Puebla* (No. 30): 24: "Poverty is the by-product of 'determinate situations and economic, social, and political structures.'"

The Bible never speaks of human rights. The rights spoken of in the Bible belong to the orphan, the widow, the pauper, the immigrant, and the alien. Biblical rights . . . are the rights of the oppressed. In the Bible the basic, electrifying assertion is, "He who oppresses the poor blasphemes his Maker, but he who is kind to the needy glorifies him" (Prov. 14:31; cf. 17:5). Everyone has someone to defend: a woman, her spouse; a man, his children; children, their parents. The poor alone have no one to look after them. And so God has taken up their cause himself. Now it is he who "executes justice for the orphan and the widow, and befriends the alien, feeding and clothing him" (Deut. 10:18; cf. Jer. 22:16; Prov. 22:22-23).[22]

This focus on the biblically based rights of the poor has taken on the name "preferential option for the poor" — a spiritual, hermeneutical, and practical privileging of the underprivileged. It demands that fellow believers stand in solidarity with the poor, sharing in their suffering, understanding their viewpoint, and seeking out their well-being.

Today many liberation theologians see the socioeconomic conditions of the poor in the Third World as parallel to those of the people of God in biblical times. According to the theology of liberation, this parallel situation permits the poor to understand the conditions of oppression described in Scripture as a very close analogue to their own. Such an analogous situation gives them a privileged position from which to understand Scripture. It also hears the cries of today's poor as echoes of those cries lifted up within the pages of Scripture.

And just as was the case in biblical times, it will be difficult to create a more just society without serious conflict. As Boff notes, this conflict is one of rights:

In Latin America, under the national security regimes in the name of the right to private property, that is, in the name of

22. Boff, *When Theology Listens to the Poor*, p. 58.

capital, all other rights are systematically violated: freedom of assembly, freedom of partisan political organization, freedom of the press and communication.[23]

But just as the plagues and the Exodus disrupted an unjust Egyptian society, so too does God's deliverance upset unjust contemporary societies when they are challenged by the gospel. Jesus took the suffering of the poor upon himself. And now Latin America and other parts of the "two-thirds world" bear that cross.[24] As Jesus took the role of the servant who suffered with the poor, those who follow him must likewise embrace those who are being crucified.[25] The end of the Christian story is not the crucifixion but the victory of resurrection and life. And those who are poor in this world or embrace the poor of this world are finally victorious in Christ. In the resurrection, the tables are turned and the downtrodden are raised up with their triumphant brother and savior.

Before moving to the Reformed tradition, I should say a few words about liberation theology and Marxism. First, there are many theologies of liberation; some of them do use Marxism as an underlying social analysis, and others do not. Second, the "option for the poor" proclaimed by liberation theology does not require either a Marxist social analysis or a Marxist implementation; it is a biblical position. Third, we should not be naïve about the social changes proposed by liberation theologians and others: their implementation would create conflict.

23. Boff, p. 44.

24. The terms "First World" (Europe and North America), "Second World" (the Eastern bloc), and "Third World" (developing nations) have become problematic and perhaps anachronistic. By the "two-thirds world" I am referring to the two-thirds of the world's population, usually in the southern hemisphere, who live in relative poverty.

25. Boff, p. 121.

The Reformed Tradition

My examination of poverty and need in the Protestant tradition begins with John Calvin. Since Calvin was not only a leading theologian of the Reformation but is also often credited with having a significant influence in Western political thought,[26] it is appropriate for us to consider his position on issues of poverty and the just distribution of goods. On the social question of poverty, Calvin begins by focusing on the theme of the image of God: he vigorously asserts that this presence of the *imago dei* in other people is, in itself, sufficient reason to come to the aid of a neighbor, no matter how despicable that neighbor may actually be. The image of God in all humans requires our highest honor and love. Calvin states this emphatically and at length:

> Scripture helps us [not to grow weary in well-doing] in the best way when it teaches that we are not to consider that merit of men themselves but to look upon the image of God in all men, to which we owe all honor and love. However, it is among members of the household of faith that this same image is more carefully to be noted [Gal. 6:10] in so far as it has been renewed and restored through the Spirit of Christ. . . . Therefore, whatever man you meet who needs your aid, you have no reason to refuse to help him. Say, 'He is a stranger', but the Lord has given him a mark that ought to be familiar to you, by virtue of the fact that he forbids you to "despise your own flesh" [Isa. 58:7, Vg.]. Say, 'He is contemptible and worthless'; but the Lord shows him to be one to whom he has deigned to give the beauty of his image. Say that you owe nothing for any service of his; but God, as it were, has put him in his own place in order that you may recognize toward him the many and great benefits with which God has bound you to himself. Say that he does not deserve even your least effort for his sake; but the image of

26. See, for example, Ernst Troeltsch's famous *Social Teachings of the Christian Churches* (New York: Harper & Row, 1960).

God, which recommends him to you, is worthy of your giving yourself and all your possessions. Now if he has not only deserved no good at your hand, but has also provoked you by unjust acts and curses, not even this is just reason why you should cease to embrace him in love and to perform the duties of love on his behalf [Matt. 6:14, 18:35; Luke 17:3].[27]

Every person, according to Calvin, must be honored, no matter how vile or undeserving he or she actually is; and that honor may even require that we give all of our possessions to him or her.[28] The image of God is so potent that no human judgment about a person's value can invalidate it.

Though Calvin never proposes Christian socialism, and indeed was among the first theologians of his age to recognize the validity of interest payments, he does advocate conditions of relative equality in which all people have their basic needs met. He also recognizes that wealth in the hands of a few can lead to oppression. For example, when commenting on Deut. 15:1 — "At the end of every seventh year you must make a remission of debts" — Calvin says:

Inasmuch as God had given them the use of the franchise [earthly possessions], the best way to preserve their liberty was by maintaining a condition of rough equality, lest a few persons of immense wealth oppress the general body. Since, therefore, the rich, if they had been permitted constantly to increase their wealth, would have tyrannized over the rest, God put a restraint on immoderate power by means of this law.[29]

27. John Calvin, *Institutes of the Christian Religion*, bk. III, ch. VII, ed. John T. McNeill, trans. Ford Lewis Battles (Philadelphia: Westminster Press, 1960), p. 696.

28. As seen in the above quote, Calvin sees the image of God as present in all, but more readily observable in the believer. The fact that the image is more obscured in unbelievers does not, however, negate our responsibilities toward them.

29. John Calvin, *The Harmony of the Last Four Books of Moses*, trans. Chas. W. Dingham (Grand Rapids: Eerdmans, 1950), eighth commandment, in Deut. 15:1, vol. X.

In his *Institutes of the Christian Religion,* Calvin's ethic focuses on self-denial, and he insists that the right to hold property is conditional on its usage for the good of others. For Calvin, proper usage of property requires a willingness to deny oneself its benefits, and use it for the sake of one's fellow.

> Scripture, to lead us by the hand to this [guide to self-denial], warns that whatever benefits we obtain from the Lord have been entrusted to us on this condition: that they be applied to the common good of the church. And therefore the lawful use of all benefits consists in a literal and kindly sharing of them with others. No surer rule and no more valid exhortation to keep it could be devised than when we are taught that all the gifts we possess have been bestowed by God and entrusted to us on condition that they be distributed for our neighbors' benefit [cf. I Peter 4:10].[30]

This economic morality is furthered by Calvin's understanding of stewardship. For Calvin, God appoints us stewards of God's goods — for the good of others:

> We are the stewards of everything God has conferred on us by which we are able to help our neighbor, and are required to render account of our stewardship. Moreover, the only right stewardship is that which is tested by the rule of love. Thus it will come about that we shall not only join zeal for another's benefit with care for our own advantage, but shall subordinate the latter to the former.[31]

In Calvin's ethic, earthly possessions are tools to be used in our practice of self-denial. The love of self must be subordinated to the love of brother and sister, and the standard by which our piety is

30. Calvin, *Institutes,* p. 695.
31. Calvin, *Institutes,* p. 695.

evaluated is that of service to the neighbor. For Calvin, obeying the law implies the duties of love. He says: "God forbids us to hurt or harm a brother unjustly, because he wills that the brother's life be dear and precious to us. So at the same time he requires those duties of love which can apply to its preservation."[32] This love of neighbor is then not only a refusal to harm the neighbor; it also requires outgoing activity that serves his or her good. In sum, Calvin sees property as a tool that must be used to perform positive good for the neighbor.

Various Protestant Traditions

Many traditions within Protestantism echo the aforementioned themes. In 1990, for example, a diverse assembly of Protestant theologians, economists, and policy-makers gathered in England to address questions of economic justice in the light of Christian faith. The document they produced, the "Oxford Declaration on Christian Faith and Economics,"[33] also emphasizes the doctrine of the "image of God." It declares: "Human beings are both part of creation and also unique. Only human beings are created in the image of God" (par. 7). The Oxford Declaration also emphasizes God's ownership of all things and the need for humans to continue to work in the world as his stewards:

> Work involves all those activities done, not for their own sake, but to satisfy human needs. Work belongs to the very purpose for which God originally made human beings. (par. 13)

---

32. *Institutes*, pp. 375-76.

33. "The Oxford Declaration on Christian Faith and Economics," in Herbert Schlossberg, Vinay Samuel, and Ronald J. Sider, eds., *Christianity and Economics in the Post–Cold War Era: The Oxford Declaration and Beyond* (Grand Rapids: Eerdmans, 1994). The Oxford Declaration was not produced by an official church body, but it was signed by more than 100 Protestant economists, theologians, philosophers, and development workers.

In the Bible and in the first centuries of the Christian tradition, meeting one's needs and the needs of one's community (especially its underprivileged members) was an essential purpose of work. (par. 16)

Echoing Leviticus 25:23, the Oxford Declaration recognizes God as the owner of all things, and humans as the managers of those things. Thus, if we follow God's will for the use of property, we will manage the land in such a way that we meet the basic needs of all people. The signatories further declare:

Justice requires conditions such that each person is able to participate in society in a way compatible with human dignity. Absolute poverty, where people lack even minimal food and housing, basic education, health care, and employment, denies people the basic economic resources necessary for just participation in the community. Corrective action with and on behalf of the poor is a necessary act of justice. This entails responsibilities for individuals, families, churches, and governments. . . . (par. 40)

In affirmation of the dignity of God's creatures, God's justice for them requires life, freedom, and sustenance. . . . Human beings therefore have a claim on other human beings for social arrangements that ensure that they have access to the sustenance that makes life in society possible. (par. 51)

Ronald Sider and Stephen Mott, two signatories of the Oxford Declaration, make a summary statement of what they believe biblical justice implies:

The traditional criterion of distributive justice, which comes closest to the biblical paradigm, is distribution according to needs. Guaranteeing basic needs for life in community becomes more important than the criteria, which are central in many worldly systems: worth, birth, social contribution, might and ability or contract.[34]

The evangelical British economist John P. Wogaman sums up his view of just distribution: "The capacity of any economic system or policy to meet the rudimentary needs of all is surely the most elementary criterion of the moral acceptability of that system or policy."[35]

A Protestant document produced by the Evangelical Lutheran Church in America sounds similar notes.[36] It affirms the image of God and the requirement that all share in the produce of the earth. "Holy Scripture declared that the earth is the Lord's and that persons created in God's image are divinely authorized to care for this earth and to share in its blessings."[37] Later it states: "Created in the image of God, persons are together stewards of God's bounty."[38] The Lutheran statement then goes on to define economic justice on the basis of the following principles.

> Economic justice denotes the fair apportioning of resources and products, of opportunities and responsibilities, of burdens and benefits among the members of a community. It includes the provision for basic human need, fair compensation for work done, and the opportunity for the full utilization of personal gifts in productive living.[39]

---

34. Stephen Mott and Ronald J. Sider, "Economic Justice: A Biblical Paradigm," in David P. Gushee, ed., *Toward a Just and Caring Society* (Grand Rapids: Baker, 1999), p. 45.

35. John P. Wogaman, "Economic Problems as Ethical Problems," in Pohier and Mieth, *Concilium: Christian Ethics and Economics* (Edinburgh: T&T Clark; New York: Seabury Press, 1980), p. 80.

36. *Economic Justice: Stewardship of Creation in Human Community*, 1993, elca.org/des. See also Max L. Stackhouse, Dennis P. McCann, and Shirley J. Roels, eds., *On Moral Business: Classical and Contemporary Resources for Ethics in Economic Life* (Grand Rapids: Eerdmans, 1995), pp. 430-34.

37. Evangelical Lutheran Church in America, in *On Moral Business*, p. 430.

38. ELCA, p. 431.

39. ELCA, p. 433.

Here justice is the provision of that which people need in order to be fully human.[40]

The United Church of Christ has also produced a document that echoes these themes.[41]

> In light of the parable of the great judgment, a just economic system fulfills the basic material needs of all members of the human community and enhances the life opportunities of the poor, the weak, and groups at the margin of society.[42]

These are examples of only a modest selection of the church documents that address the question of the right to basic sustenance.[43] As one can see in the many citations above, Roman Catholic, liberation, and various Protestant traditions all affirm a right to basic sustenance for everyone in the modern world. While each tradition affirms this with different nuances, all unite in the belief that meeting the basic needs of all people is a Christian mandate. Traditional Catholic sources point to the nature of the earth as God's creation, made for the sustenance of all, and they claim a "universal destiny for human goods." Liberation theologies emphasize God's option for the poor, as well as the concomitant requirement that Christians must also show solidarity with the needy and the oppressed. Calvin and various Protestant traditions point out that all human beings share a common nature as image-bearers of God, which merits respect and service, and they see "stewardship" as piety in action.

---

40. ELCA, p. 431.

41. *Christian Faith and Economic Life*, United Church of Christ (www.ucc.org), Audrey Chapman Smock, ed. (New York: United Church Board for World Ministries, 1987), cited in *On Moral Business*, pp. 454-67.

42. UCC, p. 457.

43. A source for a wide range of documents on this subject from churches, other religions, philosophers and economists used here is Stackhouse, McCann, and Roels, eds., *On Moral Business: Classical and Contemporary Resources for Ethics in Economic Life*.

Having built a bridge from biblical times to contemporary Christian theologies, I now turn to the question of who the poor are today.

Basic Needs

Who are the poor? In Scripture "the widow, the orphan, and the alien" was the traditional listing for the category that indicated the needy. In biblical times, each of these three groups was characterized by a lack of power and rights, due to the fact that, within ancient societies such as Israel, only free adult males had rights. Having rights, these men exercised power over and were responsible for their women, children, slaves, and foreign laborers. As a result, women and children who had been widowed or orphaned and had no adult male to stand up for them were without legal standing. They had no court of appeal. In fact, in order to present their case in court, they required the presence of an adult male advocate. Thus, when the Bible was constantly calling on Israelites to stand up for the widow, the orphan, and the alien, it was calling on those with standing and power to support those who were powerless.

Widows, orphans, and aliens are often needy and powerless even today. For example, in the United States, 36 percent of black women without husbands live below the poverty line;[44] and 37 percent of all black children under the age of five also live in poverty.[45] Yet using this biblical trio of neediness as a contemporary operational definition of the needy is problematical. Being widowed, orphaned, or an alien may or may not make one needy and powerless. We do not, for example, base qualifications for food stamps on only these three criteria. Therefore, in what follows I will advance a contemporary definition of "basic needs" that captures the sense of the ancient biblical one. It may help us identify those who fit the definition today of be-

---

44. U.S. Census Bureau, *Statistical Abstracts of the United States: 2004-2005*, 124th edition (Washington, DC), p. 455, table 690.

45. *Statistical Abstracts of the United States: 2004-2005*, p. 451, table 682.

ing needy and powerless, as did the orphan, widow, and alien in ancient Israel. This definition of poverty, which has been proposed by Amartya Sen, a Nobel laureate in economics, has gained acceptance among many economists and development theorists.

Sen's definition of poverty focuses on "functions and capabilities." By capabilities, Sen means the "ability to do valuable acts or reach valuable states of being."[46] Sen focuses on the capability of humans to function freely within their specific cultural context. Each person is an agent, and an agent must be able to act. Sen contrasts this view of "capabilities" with the mainstream economic position, which focuses on the satisfaction of preferences and income levels. Sen believes that his "'agency aspect' takes a wider view of the person [than does mainstream theory], including valuing the various things he or she would want to see happen, and the ability to form such objectives and to have them realized."[47] For Sen, economic systems are to be judged successful when they provide human agents with the capability they need to achieve crucial functionings.[48] These "functionings" may include basic physical things such as being nourished and sheltered, breathing clean air, and so forth. They may also include more abstract notions, such as possessing self-respect and dignity, participating in the life of community, and being able to appear in public without shame.

Sen recognizes that a very abstract definition of "functioning" could lead to absurd conclusions. For example, a wealthy woman may choose to fast for health or religious reasons at the same time that a poor woman does not eat because she has no food. While both do function in the same way, their capabilities are clearly different: one fasts out of choice; the other is compelled to fast.[49] The capability to achieve a particular functioning, rather than a particular func-

46. Amartya Sen, "Capability and Well-Being," in Martha Nussbaum and Amartya Sen, eds., *The Quality of Life* (Oxford: Clarendon Press, 1997), p. 30.

47. Amartya Sen, *On Ethics and Economics* (Oxford: Basil Blackwell, 1987), p. 59.

48. Amartya Sen, "Capability and Well-Being," pp. 30-53.

49. This example is from "Capability and Well-Being," p. 45.

tion, is thus the standard of judgment. More concretely, the relevant factor is that the poor woman is not able to eat and the wealthy woman is able to, not their common condition of having gone without food.

An ability to achieve functions, moreover, does not require that all people have an absolute equality of goods. Rather, differences based on cultural and personal diversity are recognized. Using this standard, Sen acknowledges that the basic needs of people in the developed world may be vastly different from those of the "two-thirds world." For example, the capacity to function as a family in the developed world might require tens of thousands of dollars per year, whereas someone in the "two-thirds world" might be capable of functioning on hundreds of dollars per year. Theologian Douglas Hicks, who has used Sen's work extensively, clarifies the relationship between equality and fairness: "Equality and difference is a false dichotomy; it is preferable to speak of basic equalities that enable genuine complex differences."[50] Hicks explains that "equality of basic capability is a necessary condition for the expression of genuine differences."[51] By this he means that basic equality is not a leveler that makes all alike; rather, it is the base potential that permits each person to develop as a distinct individual within her or his specific cultural context.

For Sen, therefore, poverty means not only that a person has a low income (as is typically understood in mainstream theory); it means that a person has a low capacity to function. A low income could be but one among many causes of this incapacity: illness, lack of clean water, oppression, and more might all be factors. Some persons may function well at an income level that would bring others to destitution. Women are more likely to be poor than men due to factors such as pregnancy, the opportunity — or lack of it — to work for pay, or the demands of their household. They may find it more

---

50. Douglas Hicks, *Inequality and Christian Ethics* (Cambridge, UK: Cambridge University Press, 2000), p. 35.
51. Hicks, p. 35.

difficult to convert a basic capability into a functioning than men do. This ability to "convert" a capability into a function is the issue that income-based definitions of poverty do not address. Sen writes,

> The conversion of income into basic capabilities may vary greatly between individuals and also between different societies, so that the ability to reach minimally acceptable levels of basic capabilities can go with varying levels of minimally adequate incomes. The income centred view of poverty, based on specifying an interpersonally invariant 'poverty line' income, may be very misleading in the identification and evaluation of poverty.[52]

Sen also challenges the assumption of mainstream economics that the satisfaction of each individual's preferences must serve as the standard definition of well-being. He recognizes that not only an individual's satisfaction but social factors must also play a part if people are to possess basic capabilities. Sen notes: "A person's ability to achieve various valuable functionings may be greatly enhanced by public action and policy. . . ."[53] Policies set in place by the government may give us the freedom to choose a life, for example, without malaria or polluted water, or with the freedom to receive a challenging education, equal opportunities in the labor market, and so forth. These public and social goods then become part of an economic system that enables people to function within that particular society.

I believe that Sen's definition of capabilities and functions can help us enact the biblical mandate of basic sustenance for all. Sen proposes that the current economic system be arranged in such a way that all are capable of functioning within their particular society. In biblical times, orphans, widows, and aliens were incapable of functioning within Israelite society. Providing people with the means to

---

52. Sen, "Capability and Well-Being," p. 41.
53. Sen, "Capability and Well-Being," p. 44.

function in their society today thus seems analogous to the biblical demand to care for the widows, orphans, and aliens of Scripture. A contemporary economic system that enables people to function within their particular cultural milieu today would be analogous to the economic system outlined in Scripture — with its commands about tithing, gleaning, and so forth. The means we use to meet needs today may vary widely from those used in ancient times, but the condition of being incapable of functioning in society carries across time.

I recognize that the poor today may require assistance in far different ways than did the poor in biblical times. This theoretical description of the poor as those incapable of functioning thus does not serve as a policy manual for contemporary relief and development work. Nevertheless, it does permit us to see who the needy are today, that is, who are in an analogous situation to the needy in ancient Israel. This leads us to the next question for this chapter. How do the covenant laws of Scripture regarding the poor relate to contemporary human rights language used in modern societies?

Rights and Responsibilities

Scripture does not use the term "human rights"; the phrase is a modern one. However, Scripture did place clear responsibilities and duties on members of Israelite society. Israel's laws showed them how to live as God's people in God's land. These covenantal laws were codified, and they were applied to all community members. As noted, these laws reflect a particular concern for the weakest members of that society. Thus when Israel failed to fulfill its responsibilities toward the poor, it was a moral failure, a legal failure, and a rupture of the covenant.

Connecting the covenant laws of Israel to contemporary rights theory will require a little translation work. In Israel each member of society had responsibilities for and duties toward other members of the community, which reflected the reality of their love toward God.

Being a citizen of a Western democracy also entails responsibilities and duties toward others in society. The individual herself has rights, and she may claim those rights over against society. Society, then, is responsible to fulfill those recognized rights. Such rights are considered "inalienable" and adhere directly to the individual. States enforce the rights of the individual, and the individual can make claims against the state.

The writings of philosopher Henry Shue[54] regarding "responsibilities and duties" will help us to relate the scriptural covenant language to contemporary human rights. Shue says that responsibilities entail corresponding duties.[55] Defining these terms, he suggests that responsibilities are broad mandates that can be enacted in numerous ways, whereas duties are specific ordinances that can only be obeyed or disobeyed. We can apply this language to describe what went on in ancient Israel. In Scripture, the responsibility to provide basic sustenance for the poor entailed various kinds of duties. The basic responsibility of Israel was to ensure that all Israelites were capable of participating in covenant society. Covenant laws then specified ways by which this would be certain to happen: Laws against theft kept property safe. Laws against moving property boundaries, using unbalanced scales, and so forth protected people from economic harm. And practices such as gleaning, giving part of the tithe to the poor, permitting the redemption of lost lands, and the broad directive to be "open-handed" toward the poor restored people to their economic place in society.

Shue argues that there are contemporary duties of this nature for our modern society that reflect our responsibility toward the poor: "1) Duties not to eliminate a person's only available means of subsistence, that is — duties to *avoid* depriving, 2) duties to *protect* people against deprivation of the only available means of subsistence by

54. Henry Shue, *Basic Rights: Subsistence, Affluence and U.S. Foreign Policy* (Princeton: Princeton University Press, 1980). Shue is the Wyn and William Y. Hutchinson Professor of Ethics and Public Life at Cornell University and was cited in the Introduction as a source for terms used.

55. Shue, *Basic Rights*, Chapter Two, "Correlative Duties," pp. 35-64.

other people, that is — duties to protect from deprivation, 3) duties to provide for the subsistence of those unable to provide for their own, that is — duties to *aid* the deprived."[56]

While the enactment of duties to avoid deprivation, protect from deprivation, and aid the deprived may be vastly different in a modern and technologically advanced society than they were in an ancient agrarian society, the responsibility nevertheless remains. In Israel, God laid a clear responsibility upon Israel to provide for the poor, the alien, and the widow. This general responsibility entailed specific correlating duties, encoded in covenant law, which served to avoid deprivation, protect from deprivation, and aid the deprived. If we accept Scripture as an expression of God's enduring will, this responsibility will remain normative among Jews and Christians. In fact, this responsibility has been accepted in many societies throughout history. Shue notes:

> Subsistence rights are in no way an original, new, or advanced idea. If subsistence rights seem strange, this is more than likely because Western liberalism has had a blind spot for severe economic need. Far from being new or advanced, subsistence rights are found in traditional societies that are often treated by modern societies as generally backward or primitive.[57]

Above, Shue notes that a response to the threat of deprivation could include avoiding deprivation, protecting from deprivation, and aiding the deprived. This is important to highlight, lest it be thought that either Shue or I is recommending vast redistributive policies.

---

56. Shue, pp. 52-53 (italics in original). Shue later reconsiders his three categories of "avoiding, protecting and aiding," agreeing with Jeremy Waldron that we might better think of "successive waves of duties." Shue, p. 160. Shue goes on further to note specific duties that the above imply, including the establishment of institutions that protect from deprivation, and aiding those who are victims of social failures or natural disasters (p. 60).

57. Shue, p. 27. See also James C. Scott, *The Moral Economy of the Peasant: Rebellion and Subsistence in Southeast Asia* (New Haven: Yale University Press, 1976).

Shue suggests that, in fact, protecting the deprived from further deprivation or loss is an early precaution that might preclude the need to provide direct aid later:

> Severe harm to some people's ability to maintain themselves can be caused by changes in the use to which other people put vital resources (like land) they control. In such cases even someone who denied that individuals or organizations have duties to supply commodities to people who are helpless to obtain them for themselves, might grant that the government ought to execute the society's duty of protecting people from having their ability to maintain their own survival destroyed by the actions of others. If this protection is provided, there will be much less need later to provide commodities themselves to compensate for deprivations.[58]

Neither Shue nor I assume that "giving a handout" should be the only method used to provide basic sustenance. It was not so in Israel, and it need not be today. Shue notes:

> The honoring of subsistence rights may often in no way involve transferring commodities to people, but may instead involve preventing people's being deprived of the commodities or the means to borrow, make, or buy the commodities. Preventing such deprivations will indeed require what can be called positive actions, especially protective and self-protective actions.[59]

I find that Shue's understanding of rights and basic sustenance also correlates with the biblical mandate of basic sustenance for all. In ancient Israel the responsibility to care for the widow, the orphan, and the alien was enacted by numerous covenant laws that helped avoid deprivation, protect from deprivation, and aid the deprived.

58. Shue, p. 45.
59. Shue, p. 51.

Today, duties to avoid deprivation, protect the deprived, and aid the deprived might be enacted in quite different ways than they were in that society. For example, avoiding deprivation may imply that we care for the natural resources in such a way that present and future generations are not deprived. Protecting the deprived may imply that we help keep people employable and employed, or seeing to it that property is protected. Aiding the deprived may be required when natural or human-made disasters strike. The biblical mandate to care for the needy remains in force. The means of enacting this mandate has undoubtedly changed.

Shue also helps us perform one more task in our process of making a biblical mandate current among modern republics. He helps us clarify how a right to basic sustenance fits within a broader theory of justice. Shue describes sustenance rights as one side of what he considers "basic rights." For Shue, "basic rights are the morality of the depths. They specify the one level beneath which no one is to be allowed to sink."[60] The other side of the basic rights coin includes the rights that provide security for life and property.[61] Without one set, the other can never be secure: I might have land but be unable to work it because I am too weak from starvation. Or, perhaps I may be able to work my land, but someone stronger than I comes and takes it. Both sides of the basic rights coin — the basic rights and the security rights — are necessary, and all people may claim these basic rights. "Basic rights," says Shue, "are everyone's minimum reasonable demands upon the rest of humanity."[62]

For Shue, other rights, such as those of commutative justice, are secondary. He urges that "security rights and subsistence rights are parallel inasmuch as both are required if one is to enjoy secondary rights."[63] Shue believes that the relationship between basic rights and secondary rights is this: "If a right is basic, other, non-basic rights may be sacrificed, if necessary, in order to secure the basic right. But

60. Shue, p. 18.
61. Shue, *Basic Rights*, Chapter One — "Security and Subsistence."
62. Shue, p. 19.
63. Shue, p. 26.

the protection of a basic right may not be sacrificed in order to secure the enjoyment of a non-basic right."[64]

Bringing together the biblical mandate of basic sustenance for all with the rights language of Henry Shue, we find that basic sustenance appears to be a basic moral right. It is one side of a basic rights package that includes the rights to personal liberty and personal property. In a way that may parallel Scripture, Shue holds that all people may demand basic sustenance from their societies.

Conclusion

Finally, having crossed these bridges, where have we arrived? I believe we have arrived at a place where we can make three statements about the biblical mandate of basic sustenance for all in contemporary societies. First, we can say that contemporary Christian theology affirms and amplifies that mandate. Second, we can say that economic theory such as that of Amartya Sen provides us with a way forward in describing and defining what basic needs are. Third, we can say that sustenance is a basic right that entails corresponding duties for contemporary societies.

64. Shue, p. 19.

CHAPTER SIX

Distributing Benefits and Burdens according to "Spheres"

When it is a question of money, everybody is of the same religion.

Voltaire

Distributive Justice and Contemporary Theory

The task I have taken up in this book is to provide flesh for Ulpian's bare-bones statement that "justice is giving each his due" in such a way that basic human needs are met. And the contexts for our investigation have been the biblical and Christian teachings on poverty and contemporary market economics. In the preceding chapter I showed that the mandate of basic sustenance for all that is found in the Bible can be brought forward into contemporary society. The Christian tradition also challenges any system of distributive justice that only rewards economic contributors, demanding in addition that all of God's image-bearers have basic human necessities. The Bible and the Christian tradition say that we are all related to others as part of the same family of God-imagers. All humans are inherently needy and must have their basic needs met if they are to be full participants in their societies.

This claim is based, theologically, on the nature of humanity and on the divinely authored purposes of creation. The Christian tradition claims that all human persons are inestimably valuable, regardless of what property they might possess or how much they might contribute to a productive enterprise. Thus the shoeless child of a Mexican migrant worker in Texas is just as valuable in God's sight — and therefore in ours — as the CEO of the supermarket chain that sells the produce that migrant worker picks. The goods of creation are destined for all of needy humanity, not only those who happen to hold property or achieve economically valuable goals.

In the second chapter we saw that, in order for a market economy to function, it requires that people have the political right to hold property and the commutative right to contractual exchange. The first right (property) is based on equal standing before the law: all citizens have an equal right to hold property. The second set of rights is based on contribution: those who contribute to marginal productivity deserve proportional compensation. In the third chapter we saw, however, that a normally functioning market, as understood and elaborated in mainstream economic theory, will not necessarily provide basic sustenance for all, such as is demanded in Christian Scripture and tradition. Capitalism, as conceptualized in mainstream economic theory, is not designed to respond to claims based on the criterion of need. Rather, it responds to claims based on effective demand among property-holders. I have shown that while capitalism requires two kinds of rights in order to function effectively — commutative rights and political (especially property) rights — it does not recognize the moral right based on need.

What is required, then, is a system of distributive justice that will incorporate all three kinds of moral claims: the political rights that protect life and property, the right to basic sustenance, and commutative rights. The first set of rights, the political rights, protects goods and the people who hold them. The second set of rights, basic sustenance rights, permits people to participate in their society. The final set of rights, commutative rights, provides guarantees necessary for people to engage in economic exchange. A theory of justice that combines all three of these aspects can potentially establish a state of affairs in which people may be provided what is due to them on all relevant bases: equality, need, and contribution. It can honor the biblical demand that all persons have basic sustenance. To do so, it must incorporate — but go beyond — the system of distributive justice provided within the free market alone.

The system I wish to present now shows how these three kinds of claims might interrelate within democratic societies. It is particularly indebted to two thinkers: turn-of-the-twentieth-century theologian and statesman Abraham Kuyper (1837-1920) and contemporary political theorist Michael Walzer (b. 1935). In this chapter I will describe the political and theological framework of each thinker; together they incorporate the three kinds of claims mentioned above. Kuyper and Walzer can help us clarify when claims based on need are legitimate, how different spheres of justice interrelate, and what standards for distribution might apply within these spheres. My goal is to show that claims to human goods based on need are appropriate in one particular sphere, and that they need not conflict with the commutative justice found in a free market.

Kuyper and Walzer may seem to be an unlikely pair. Kuyper was a man of the nineteenth century and Walzer of the twentieth; Kuyper was a vigorous Calvinist, and Walzer is a Jew;[1] Kuyper was a prime minister of the Netherlands, and Walzer is an American democratic socialist. Nevertheless, both seek a balanced system of justice that recognizes the diversity of human life; both are convinced that political theories that derive rights from only the state or the individual are inadequate; and both use the concept of "spheres" as a construct to judge the legitimacy of particular moral claims in particular areas of life. The issues that both thinkers address are broader than the specific problematic of the right to basic sustenance; nevertheless, their conceptualization of "spheres of justice" is capable of respond-

---

1. Walzer clearly affirms his Jewish identity; see, e.g., Michael Walzer, "Blacks and Jews: A Personal Reflection," in Jack Salzman and Cornel West, eds., *Struggles in the Promised Land* (New York: Oxford University Press, 1997).

ing to the specific claim of basic sustenance for all humans. I wish to show that a fruitful blend of Kuyper and Walzer can provide a platform on which we may build a proposal for distributive justice that honors the biblical mandate of basic sustenance for all.

Abraham Kuyper

Abraham Kuyper was a "mountainous figure in the small, flat country of The Netherlands."[2] He was a theologian, an orator, an editor, the founder of both a daily newspaper and a weekly church newspaper, the founder and president of the Free University of Amsterdam, a member of parliament, prime minister of the Netherlands (1901-1905), and father of eight. During his lifetime he shaped that nation. And since his death, his writings have continued to wield influence in other regions where Reformed Christians gather, including the United States, Canada, South Africa, Great Britain, western Africa, and Australia. Kuyper is of special interest to this study because of his theory of "sphere sovereignty," which he developed as a scholar and attempted to put into practice as a politician.

Like Adam Smith's work, Kuyper's thought and practice unite religion, economic theory, and political practice. And like Smith's thought, too, political rights, personal values, and religion coordinate and complement each other — rather than oppose each other. But unlike Smith, Kuyper was specifically and resolutely Christian in his basic principles. He attempted to follow these principles in all his thinking and politicking. Princeton ethicist Max Stackhouse puts it this way:

2. This witty description of Kuyper (a portly man) is from James Bratt. Numerous works have appeared on Kuyper's life and thought. The classic biography is by P. Kastreel, *Abraham Kuyper* (Kampen: Kok, 1938). Good recent works in English on Kuyper include Peter S. Heslam, *Creating a Christian Worldview: Abraham Kuyper's "Lectures on Calvinism"* (Grand Rapids: Eerdmans, 1998) and John Bolt, *A Free Church, A Holy Nation* (Grand Rapids: Eerdmans, 2001). A review of recent literature on Kuyper can be found in James D. Bratt, "In the Shadow of Mt. Kuyper: A Survey of the Field," *Calvin Theological Journal* 31, no. 1 (Apr. 1996): 51-66.

He [Kuyper] held that it is a serious error to say that Christianity has, or should have, no implications for the organization of the common life or that it pertains only to spiritual yearnings seated in the heart or expressed in the privacy of the prayer group; or that society is best ordered by a secular, pragmatic politics that avoids religions wherever possible. On the contrary, the well-being of the soul, the character of local communities, the fabric of the society at large, and the fate of civilization are intimately related and cannot be separated from theological and moral issues.[3]

Before delving into Kuyper's theological and political theory and its contribution to the questions of distributive justice, I will briefly note the context out of which Kuyper's thinking grew. Kuyper was the son of a Calvinist pastor, but he migrated intellectually into theological liberalism while pursuing a doctorate in theology at the University of Leyden. After earning this degree, he went on to be the pastor of a rural congregation, and while serving this church he was "converted" by his peasant parishioners to a more orthodox form of Calvinism.[4] Throughout his career as both a theologian and a politician, Kuyper would navigate intellectually and politically between the poles of his more liberal teachers and his conservative church members: he found the theology of the former to be groundless and the social policy of the latter to be fruitless or reactionary. His career in both politics and theology, therefore, moved between these positions, sometimes chastening one or the other, and sometimes forming alliances with them.[5]

3. Max Stackhouse, "Preface," in Luis Lugo, ed., *Religion, Pluralism, and Public Life: Abraham Kuyper's Legacy for the Twenty-First Century* (Grand Rapids: Eerdmans, 2000), p. xiii.

4. James Bratt recounts this in "Abraham Kuyper: His World and Work," in James Bratt, ed., *Abraham Kuyper: A Centennial Reader* (Grand Rapids: Eerdmans, 1998), pp. 1-16. This change occurred for Kuyper in the village of Beesd in 1863-67.

5. Interestingly, he also formed political alliances with Dutch Catholics, who shared many similar concerns and inclinations. His rise to prime minister would not have taken place without this alliance. On this subject, see Bolt, *A Free Church, A Holy Nation* for both a depiction of Kuyper's political thought and practice and for

Meanwhile, other intellectuals within the broader European community during this period were developing social and political theories that would respond to their various national ambitions. In very broad terms, two routes predominated. The first was an autonomous individualism ensuing from the French Revolution, whose cry "No god, no master!" was still echoing throughout Europe during Kuyper's time. It asserted the absolute rights of the individual, as well as freedom from all other powers not authorized by the individual, especially the church and the monarchy. The other option was a unifying Idealist vision of German origin. This option viewed the nation as one spiritual and racial unity, which was then expressed in a form of state socialism. Kuyper called the French option "popular sovereignty," and he labeled the German option "state sovereignty."[6] He rejected both.[7]

In rejecting the Germanic state socialist option, Kuyper wrote: "The state may never become an octopus, which stifles the whole of life. It must occupy its own place, on its own root, among all the other trees of the forest, and thus it has to honor and maintain every form of life which grows independently in its own sacred autonomy."[8] James Skillen, a political theorist in the Kuyperian tradition, describes Kuyper's critique of state socialism in this way:

Bolt's attempt to put Kuyper's thinking in dialogue with contemporary evangelical public theology.

6. Abraham Kuyper, *Lectures on Calvinism* (Grand Rapids: Eerdmans, 1931), pp. 78-109.

7. Kuyper was certainly not the only one in Europe to address this dilemma. In particular, the parallel Roman Catholic doctrine of subsidiarity began to develop at the same time. For a comparison of subsidiarity and sphere sovereignty, see, e.g., Paul Sigmund, "Subsidiarity, Solidarity and Liberation: Alternative Approaches in Catholic Social Thought," in Lugo, ed., *Religion, Pluralism and Public Life*. See also Jonathan Chaplin, "Subsidiarity and Sphere Sovereignty: Catholic and Reformed Conceptions of the Role of the State," in Francis P. McHugh and Samuel M. Natale, eds., *Things Old and New: Catholic Social Teaching Revisited* (Lanham, MD: University Press of America, 1993).

8. James Skillen, "Introduction," in Abraham Kuyper, *The Problem of Poverty*, ed. James Skillen (Grand Rapids: Baker, 1991), p. 96.

Kuyper used the term "organic" together with the idea of diverse spheres of society, to affirm the social character of human life, with its built-in obligations of mutual accountability, trust and service. Kuyper's critique of socialism, in both its social democratic and state socialist forms, warns of the danger of reducing society to the state or the state to society. The organic character of society can be truly healthy and just only when its real diversity is preserved.[9]

For Kuyper, then, the state is not the totality of society, nor is it the only or final power in society. Instead, it is the regulative institution within society that respects the roles and authorities of other parts of the organism. Kuyper also rejected popular sovereignty:

> In the Christian religion, authority and freedom are bound together by the deeper principle that everything in creation is subject to God. The French Revolution threw out the majesty of the Lord in order to construct an artificial authority based on individual free will. . . . The Christian religion seeks personal human dignity in the social relationships of an organically integrated society. The French Revolution disturbed that organic tissue, broke those social bonds, and left nothing but the monotonous, self-seeking individual asserting his own self-sufficiency.[10]

For the purposes of this book's argument, it is worth noting how closely Kuyper's description and critique of "popular sovereignty" matches my own description and critique of mainstream economic theory. For Kuyper, the French Revolution's depiction of the human being is one of a "monotonous, self-seeking individual asserting his own self-sufficiency." A "monotonous" creature can play or sing but one tone. So, too, the individual in mainstream economic theory is always a rational "self-maximizer." All human action is predicated

9. Skillen, "Introduction," *The Problem of Poverty*, p. 21.
10. Kuyper, *The Problem of Poverty*, pp. 43-44.

on the same basis — the maximization of the utility of an individual.[11] Kuyper opposed such an individualistic and rationalistic anthropology. For him, popular sovereignty, like mainstream economic theory, meant that each person asserts his own self-sufficiency and that the social good is merely a composite of individual goods, never a common good that reaches beyond the individual. From his critique of popular sovereignty, we may deduce that Kuyper rejected one of mainstream economic theory's intellectual ancestors.

In place of either popular sovereignty or state sovereignty, Kuyper proposed a model of "sphere sovereignty." Using the Calvinist doctrine of common grace, Kuyper argued that the one God freely creates and rules all things, including a wide variety of social institutions and intellectual pursuits. God's grace and God's thoughts are found not only in the salvific work of Christ, but in all aspects of creation.

> If thinking is first in God, and if everything created is considered to be only the outflowing of God's thought so that all things have come into existence by the Logos — i.e. by divine reason or better, by the Word — yet still have their own being, then God's thinking must be contained in all things. There is nothing in the whole creation that is not the expression, the embodiment, the revelation of a thought of God.[12]

"Thinking God's thoughts after him," then, becomes not only the task of the theologian but of each believer in every sphere of life. Each sphere of life reflects the presence of the Word of God and is directly responsible to God for its being and continued existence. Each sphere of life was created by the Word of God and forms part of the continuously developing order of creation. For Kuyper, there are many "spheres":

11. Some theorists, such as Gary Becker and Richard Posner, attempt to extend this market theory into all spheres of life, while others seem content to let the theory serve only as a norm for specifically economic decisions.

12. Abraham Kuyper, "Common Grace in Science," in James D. Bratt, ed., *Abraham Kuyper: A Centennial Reader,* p. 443.

There are in life as many spheres as there are constellations in the sky and the circumference of each has been drawn on a fixed radius from the center of a unique principle, namely, the apostolic injunction *(hekastos en toi idioi tagmati)* "each in its own order" (I Cor. 15:23). Just as we speak of a 'moral world,' a 'scientific world,' a 'business world,' the 'world of art,' so we can more properly speak of a 'sphere' of morality, of the family, of social life, each with its own domain. And because each comprises its own domain, each has its own Sovereign within its bounds.[13]

Explicating sphere sovereignty, Reformed theologian Gordon Spykman says: "Each sphere has its own identity, its own unique task, its own God-given prerogatives. On each God has conferred its own peculiar right of existence and reason for existence."[14] All things are allotted their space in Kuyper's model, and the whole scheme of things is divinely ordered. But there are not "spiritual" spheres and "secular" spheres. Rather, all human efforts to develop culture are spiritual, inasmuch as every sphere finds its origin and destiny in the word of its Creator.

In a sentence that Kuyperians are fond of quoting, Kuyper says: "No single piece of our mental world is to be hermetically sealed off from the rest, and there is not a square inch in the whole domain of our human existence over which Christ, who is Sovereign over all, does not cry: 'Mine!' "[15] For Kuyper, each sphere of life has its own legitimacy and its own nature, which in turn responds in either faith or unbelief to Christ's claim as its Lord. Therefore, no sphere is more spiritual or noble than any other. Participating in family life, in eco-

13. Kuyper, "Sphere Sovereignty," in Bratt, p. 467. (I grant that Kuyper's exegesis of that text is a bit of a stretch, but I cite him on this point to show his understanding of what he called the "creation order.")

14. Gordon Spykman, "Sphere Sovereignty in Calvin and the Calvinist Tradition," in David Holwerda, ed., *Exploring the Heritage of John Calvin* (Grand Rapids: Baker, 1976), p. 167.

15. Kuyper, "Sphere Sovereignty," in Bratt, p. 488.

nomic life, in political life, or in sports are all ways of potentially fulfilling the cultural mandate to "till the earth and keep it" (Gen. 2:15). Each parcel of earth is to be cultivated in such a way that the Creator will eventually smile and say, "Well done, good and faithful servant." Humans as stewards use their unique creative gifts to work within different spheres, in accordance with their talents and in respect to the nature of each particular sphere. Each society's accumulation of these labors results in diverse human culture.[16] Thus human work, when properly directed, has social and cultural results.[17] It also has a profound religious goal: the glorification of God and service to the neighbor.

Thus the task of believers in all walks of life is to exercise their calling within their chosen sphere(s) of work; and individuals may participate in multiple spheres of life. Using an example from art history, James Bratt says:

> Kuyper would shudder at both the subject and style of Picasso's definitively modernist *Les Demoiselles d'Avignon,* but he would envision their more seemly counterpart, the Calvinist matron, as simultaneously a family member, reader, believer, consumer, patriot, teacher — each role having its own independent integrity, all cohering together in her subjective being.[18]

---

16. As Reformed theologian Henry Van Til puts it: "Culture is any and all human effort and labor expended upon the cosmos, to unearth its treasures and its riches and bring them into the service of man for the enrichment of human existence unto the glory of God." Van Til, *The Calvinistic Concept of Culture* (Grand Rapids: Baker, 1959; reprinted, with a foreword by Richard Mouw, 2001), p. 29.

17. I take "work" here to be more and better than the sheer toil that permits mere existence. Though work may involve a paying job, I take it also to include some kind of creative response to the mandate to "till and keep the earth" (Gen. 2:15) through which humans as "re-creators" may flourish. For a famous treatment of the nature of work and society that distinguishes among labor, work, and action, see Hannah Arendt, *The Human Condition* (Chicago: University of Chicago Press, 1958).

18. James D. Bratt, "Abraham Kuyper: Puritan, Victorian, Modern," in Luis E. Lugo, ed., *Religion, Pluralism, and Public Life,* p. 14.

At the center of her subjective being would be her faith, since all of life is an outworking of one's basic religious commitment. Skillen says: "For Kuyper, religion is not one thing among many that autonomous people choose to do; it is, rather, the direction that human life takes as people give themselves over to the gripping power of either the true God or false gods."[19] Hence all of life ultimately becomes service to God — or else to false gods.

What advantages, then, does the concept of sphere sovereignty have over popular or state sovereignty when it comes to the question of distributive justice? The principal advantage over both other options is that, within sphere sovereignty, neither the state nor the church, neither the market nor the president — nor anything besides God alone — may become absolute. Advocates of state sovereignty attempt to effect societal unity on the basis of some form of nationalist ideology, whereas advocates of popular sovereignty make the composite will of autonomous individuals the absolute good. Kuyper's sphere sovereignty, on the other hand, acknowledges the rights of the individual and those of the various spheres of social life. However, it subjects both individuals and institutions to normative standards derived from God's Word. This theory is thus permeable and open: each sphere can interact with the others, and all are open to influences from outside themselves. The sphere of economics, for example, will be open to influences from family or ecology, as well as claims based on need that are derived from religious beliefs. The second advantage of Kuyper's system cuts in the other direction: it declares that each sphere is genuine, legitimate, and inviolable in its own right. Institutions such as church or state are not needed to validate other spheres of life, including the economic sphere, since each sphere is already an integral part of creation.[20] All spheres derive their legitimacy from the Creator alone. Kuyper's view thus rules out an absolutizing of the church, the state, or the individual. It removes the likelihood that any

19. Skillen, "Introduction," *The Problem of Poverty*, p. 17.

20. As an illustration of this, note Kuyper's establishment of the Free University. He expended considerable labor to assure that this university would be free from controls of either his church or his state.

form of state socialism, or individualistic libertarianism, or any other totalizing ideology should gain ascendancy.

In Kuyper's theory, the relationship between the state and the other social spheres is clearly laid out. On the one hand, as quoted above, the state is never to become an "octopus," taking over roles that are rightfully accomplished in other spheres. On the other hand, the state has three important positive roles vis-à-vis the other spheres. Following his "octopus" comment, Kuyper asks rhetorically:

> Does this mean that the government has no right *whatever* of interference in these autonomous spheres of life? Not at all.
>
> It possesses the threefold right and duty: 1. Whenever different spheres clash, to compel mutual regard for the boundary-lines of each; 2. to defend individuals and the weak ones, in those spheres, against the abuse of power of the rest; and 3. to coerce all together to bear *personal* and *financial* burdens for the maintenance of the natural unity of the state.[21]

Kuyper thus envisions an activist state. Notice that all three of his positive state functions relate to economics. The first sets up boundaries between economics and other spheres in such a way that might prohibit, for example, the economic sphere from taking over the sphere of family life. The second role has direct affinities with an option for the poor. The third role recognizes the legitimate power of the state to act in favor of the social unity and good.[22] In all three of these activities we see that the state does more than prevent harm by protecting persons and property. Rather, we find an active state that defends the weak, limits the scope of various societal powers, and coerces support for the common good. Herman Dooyeweerd, a philosopher who followed Kuyper at the Free University, also saw posi-

21. Kuyper, *Lectures on Calvinism*, p. 97 (italics in original).

22. Here Kuyper seems to be using the term "state" where we would more likely say "society," as the following discussion will bear out. Kuyper also quickly adds that the state must not act unilaterally, but that each citizen has a legitimate right to his own "purse." Kuyper, *Lectures on Calvinism*, p. 97.

tive roles for government in which the state creates conditions of justice, even compelling private associations to provide just conditions within their own sphere.[23] Kuyper grounds his proposal for the inviolable legitimacy of each sphere, as well as the legitimacy of state power, by tying both to a belief in the absolute sovereignty of God.[24]

Kuyper also envisions important social and even economic roles for the church. He sees the church performing three activities that directly affect socioeconomic conditions: (1) through the exposition of the Word of God, the church challenges the rich and comforts the poor; (2) the church's function of charity demands that goods be shared so that no believer suffers want; and (3) the church brings about an equality within society that is symbolized at the communion table.[25] Note how these three tasks support claims based on need as well as equality. First, following Calvin, the church challenges those who have received much to use their goods in service of those who have little. Second, Kuyper insists that some distribution occur on the basis of need.[26] Finally, the basic equality among humans seen at the communion table serves as grounds for greater material equality in society. In sum, the church's focus on the "spiritual" does not imply that it has nothing to say about how goods should be distributed.

As noted above, the believer could simultaneously be a member of a church, a citizen of a state, and a participant in any number of social spheres. In all these aspects of life, the basic convictions of the

---

23. "Dooyeweerd acknowledges that the idea of a state that promotes 'public social justice' requires an active role of the government in civil society. According to Dooyeweerd, this implies that the government should create conditions in which citizens and private associations can enjoy their rights and carry out their duties. If private associations do not fulfill their responsibilities, he argues, the state ultimately should fulfill these tasks for the sake of public social justice." Henk Woldring, "Multiform Responsibility and the Revitalization of Civil Society," in Lugo, *Religion, Pluralism, and Public Life*, p. 187.

24. Kuyper, *Lectures on Calvinism*, p. 98.

25. Kuyper, *The Problem of Poverty*, p. 41.

26. Following Calvin, Kuyper seems to have in mind the needs of his fellow believers as a first responsibility, followed by those outside of his faith community.

Christian faith would direct the believer's activities, and she would live out her faith in whatever sphere of life she chose to engage. Permit me a word picture to describe how Kuyper's system might appear (my own image, but one I think Kuyper might have liked). Imagine that a prism has refracted light into its multiple colors: these colors represent the various social spheres of human existence — family, business, club, academy, and so forth. On one side of the colored lights stand the churches, guiding their members in the knowledge of God, which informs (but does not dictate) the basic convictions of each believer. On the other side of the spectrum stands the state, regulating the interactions among the spheres, assuring that the weak are not trampled, and calling on all persons to contribute to the common good. Neither church nor state defines the role of each sphere; instead, each derives its legitimacy and its role from God.

Having presented this general sketch of Kuyper's theory of sphere sovereignty, I turn briefly to the possible role of economic rights within his system.[27] Kuyper was a champion of liberties in two ways: he sought liberty of conscience for all, and he also sought liberty for the various institutions that operate within their particular spheres. At the same time, however, he was quite wary of economic power struggles and the potential inequities inherent in capitalism, especially those that resulted from increased industrialization throughout western Europe. In the 1890s, Kuyper was becoming an internationally recognized theologian and politician. Attempting to score points for his recently formed "Anti-revolutionary party," he gave a speech to the Christian Social Congress entitled "The Social Problem and the Christian Religion," which is an extended critique of economic injustice.[28] In it he says, for example:

27. It is interesting to note that *Lectures on Calvinism* includes chapters on religion, politics, science, and art, but none on economics.

28. Later translated into English by James W. Skillen as *The Problem of Poverty* (Grand Rapids: Baker, 1991). Kuyper would become prime minister of the Netherlands in 1901, a decade after this speech. Interestingly, Pope Leo XIII issued his landmark encyclical *Rerum Novarum* in the following year. Clearly, the social problems of workers in Europe were a motivation to both.

Where our father in heaven wills with divine generosity that an abundance of food grows from the ground, we are without excuse if, through our fault, this rich bounty is divided so unequally that one is surfeited with bread while another goes with an empty stomach to his pallet, and sometimes must even go without a pallet.[29]

He also clearly recognized that poverty was not a "spiritual" problem, solvable through an increase in piety, but a social and political problem requiring structural changes:

Whenever one uses the phrase 'social question,' one recognizes, in the most general sense, that serious doubt has arisen about the soundness of the social structure in which we live. . . . Only one thing is necessary if the social question is to exist for you: you must realize the untenability of the present state of affairs, and you must account for this untenability not by incidental causes but by a fault in the very foundation of our society's organization. If you do not acknowledge this and think that social evil can be exorcised through an increase in piety, or through friendlier treatment or more generous charity, then you may believe that we face a religious question or possibly a philanthropic question, but you will not recognize the *social* question.[30]

Kuyper's theory of sphere sovereignty was an attempt to address this kind of social and structural problem. I believe that Kuyper's model does provide direction for today. But to fill in his outline and make it understandable in terms of current discussions on human rights, I want to bring Kuyper into conversation with contemporary rights concepts. To do so, I turn to a contemporary political theorist, Michael

29. *The Problem of Poverty*, p. 61. In Kuyper's time, the "social problem" was the problem of poverty and the related issue of class struggle that arose under conditions of the industrial revolution.

30. Kuyper, *The Problem of Poverty*, pp. 50-51 (italics in original).

Walzer, whose work in important respects seems to further the conceptual framework provided by Kuyper nearly one hundred years earlier.

Michael Walzer

Contemporary political theorist Michael Walzer has proposed a pluralistic theory of justice that is in many ways complementary to that of Kuyper.[31] Walzer's now famous "spheres of justice" is a response to the Libertarian theory put forward by Robert Nozick.[32] For Nozick and others in strong libertarian traditions, claims to goods can be made only on the basis of current property rights; these claims then take priority over any claims made by the state or other social institutions.[33] Insofar as Walzer critiques Nozick, he also responds to a theory of distributive justice based purely on free-market exchange. In *Spheres of Justice,* Walzer observes that contribution to productivity is not the only grounds that justifies claims to the distribution of

31. I find no references to Kuyper in any of Walzer's writings. In addition to the works by Walzer cited in this volume, I have consulted his *Revolution of the Saints: A Study in the Origins of Radical Politics* (Cambridge, MA: Harvard Univ. Press, 1965) for possible references to Kuyper. But it is worth noting that, while there may be no direct connection, both writers are deeply grounded in Hebrew Scripture.

32. Walzer, *Spheres of Justice: A Defense of Pluralism and Equality* (New York: Basic Books, 1983). Walzer is editor of *Dissent* and has written a number of books and numerous articles, e.g., "Philosophy and Democracy," *Political Theory* 9 (1981): 379-99; "Liberalism and the Art of Separation," *Political Theory* 12 (1984); *The Company of Critics* (New York: Basic Books, 1989); "Objectivity and Social Meaning," in Martha Nussbaum and Amartya Sen, eds., *The Quality of Life* (Oxford: Clarendon Press, 1992); "Exclusion, Injustice and the Democratic State," *Dissent* 40 (1993): 55-64; *On Toleration* (New Haven: Yale University Press, 1997). Walzer's work has spawned responses at both the popular and the academic levels, e.g., in *New York Review of Books* 30, no. 12 (July 1983) and *Philosophical Quarterly* 42 (1992): 161-81. See the volume by Michael Walzer and David Miller, *Pluralism, Justice, and Equality* (Oxford: Oxford University Press, 1995). For a recent update of the dialogue, see also Michael Haus, *Die Politische Philosophie Michael Walzer: Kritik, Gemeinschaft, Gerechtigkeit* (Wiesbaden: Westdeutscher Verlag, 2000), which includes a critical bibliography.

33. Robert Nozick, *Anarchy, State and Utopia* (Oxford: Blackwell, 1974).

human goods. In fact, there are numerous criteria used to legitimate the distribution of different kinds of goods, and these criteria shift over time, and from culture to culture.[34]

For Walzer, goods and services are not like berries growing in the meadow that can be picked by any passerby; rather, they are culturally produced and defined products that gain both their meaning and their value within a particular cultural setting. For Walzer, it is fruitless to attempt to determine an abstract distributional methodology for various goods apart from the setting in which they are actually found and distributed. Theories of distribution must therefore be concretely historical. Walzer critiques efforts to provide a supracultural theory of distributive justice.

> The effort to produce a complete account of justice or a defense of equality by multiplying rights soon makes a farce of what it multiplies. To say of whatever we think people ought to have that they have a right to have it is not to say very much. Men and women do indeed have rights beyond life and liberty, but these do not follow from our common humanity; they follow from shared conceptions of social goods; they are local and particular in character.[35]

I disagree with Walzer in one way here: I believe that rights beyond life and liberty do in fact arise from our common humanity. But I will come back to this point later, when I bring Walzer into dialogue with Kuyper. What I wish to pursue here is Walzer's argument that it is the nature of the goods themselves, within their cultural context, that determines the criteria for their distribution. Each society determines both the nature of the goods and the appropriate pattern for their distribution. "Distributions are patterned in accordance with shared conceptions of what the goods are and what they are for."[36]

34. Walzer, *Spheres*, p. 6.
35. Walzer, *Spheres*, p. xv.
36. Walzer, *Spheres*, p. 7.

Thus, Walzer proposes the following theoretical framework for recognizing the nature of goods and the standards for their distribution:

1. Goods have shared meanings and values that are derived from culture.
2. Men and women take on concrete identities because of the way they conceive and create, and then possess and employ, social goods.
3. There is no single set of primary or basic goods conceivable across all moral and material worlds.
4. It is the meaning of goods that determines their movement.
5. Social meanings are historical in character; and so distributions — and just and unjust distributions — change over time.
6. When meanings are distinct, distributions must be autonomous. Every social good or set of goods constitutes, as it were, a distributive sphere within which only certain criteria and arrangements are appropriate.[37]

In this last point, Walzer proposes the concept of "spheres" as a means of determining patterns of distribution. He proposes that each sphere is characterized by the particular set of goods within it, which must then be distributed according to culturally determined criteria. Throughout history, criteria for distribution have included: physical strength, familial reputation, office, land ownership, capital, technical knowledge, and so on.[38] Distributive justice, for Walzer, requires that the criterion for the distribution of a particular good match the kind of good in question within a particular society.

> Every criterion that has any force at all meets the general rule within its own sphere, and not elsewhere. This is the effect of the rule: different goods to different companies of men and

37. *Spheres*, pp. 7-10.
38. *Spheres*, p. 11.

women for different reasons and in accordance with different procedures. And to get all this right, or to get it roughly right, is to map out the entire social world.[39]

In Walzer's view, justice occurs when goods are distributed according to locally appropriate criteria of distribution; injustice occurs when the criterion for distribution is not appropriate to the kind of good being distributed, or when one type of goods can be garnered with resources that cross the borders of its sphere. Walzer provides a few quick examples of such "trespassing": "Wealth is seized by the strong, honor by the wellborn, office by the well educated."[40] Simony (paying money for an ecclesiastical office) is a classic example of such boundary crossing: the standard for distributing goods in the sphere of the marketplace (i.e., money) is wrongly used as the standard for distributing a very different type of good, spiritual authority, in a very different sphere (i.e., ecclesiastical).[41] Walzer notes that Pascal recognized this problem long ago when he said: "Tyranny is the wish to obtain by one means what can only be had by another. We owe different duties to different qualities: love is the proper response to charm, fear to strength, and belief to learning."[42] It is certainly proper for people to dominate in a given sphere based on the criterion appropriate to that sphere; for example, the strong and speedy ought to dominate in sports, or the lovely in pageants of beauty. However, it is improper for a good to be distributed according to an unrelated criterion. As Walzer points out, "To convert one good into another, when there is no intrinsic connection between the two, is to invade the sphere where another company of men and women properly rules."[43]

Walzer views money as the chief trespasser in contemporary societies: "Money seeps across all boundaries — this is the primary form

39. *Spheres*, p. 26.
40. *Spheres*, p. 12.
41. *Spheres*, pp. 9-10.
42. Blaise Pascal, *Pensées*, trans. J. M. Cohen (Harmondsworth edition, 1961), p. 96 (no. 244); cited in *Spheres*, p. 18.
43. Walzer, *Spheres*, p. 19.

of illegal immigration; and just where one ought to try to stop it is a question of expediency as well as of principle."[44] For Walzer, justice requires that boundaries between spheres be defended against trespassers, so that the appropriate criterion for distribution within each is maintained. To defend the integrity of each sphere, we must know which criterion is being used for distribution within it. In Walzer's view, there are three criteria for making distributions within the various spheres: need, desert, and equality.[45]

Focusing on the criterion of *need,* Walzer believes that no single master list of basic needs can be created, since societies define goods and needs in reference to their own particular cultural and political settings. Nevertheless, agreements can be made within a defined community to distribute some goods on the basis of need.[46] Societies can enact agreements that determine which needs are to be fulfilled and what kind of redistribution will bring it about. Such a redistribution should occur "in accordance with some shared understanding of their needs, subject to ongoing political determination in detail."[47] As an example of this kind of redistribution, consider what occurs in families: if an older child needs a larger lunch than a younger one, the parent will pack the needed but unequal quantity of lunch for each child. Societies also meet the differing needs of their members with unequal distributions — be it for food, ceremonial garb, access to burial sites, and so forth. Within Western society, Walzer believes, redistributing according to basic needs may require the distribution of a minimal amount of money that permits active participation in society.[48]

The second criterion, *desert,* implies entitlement on the basis of some observable grounds: I am entitled to a new suit jacket, for example, because I can pay the price that is asked for it. Or I am entitled to

44. *Spheres,* p. 22.

45. *Spheres,* p. 21.

46. Walzer also observes that community membership itself, e.g., citizenship, is a good that is distributed on the basis of particular criteria within particular countries. *Spheres,* p. 29.

47. *Spheres,* p. 82.

48. *Spheres,* p. 105.

a given wage because I have performed the tasks required of the job. This criterion rules the marketplace. Walzer notes that entitlement on the basis of desert depends on many factors, especially the actual state of the economy.[49] However, as long as the merchant is selling legally marketable goods (not, for example, body parts), he or she is functioning properly in the sphere of the marketplace. Desert is the proper standard of distribution within business; and justice is served when the nature and amount of the desert is fitting to the achievement.

As noted above, the inherent problem with money as a measure of desert is that it tends to invade the other spheres. Walzer says that, given complete rein, "a radically laissez-faire economy would be like a totalitarian state, invading every other sphere, dominating every other distributive process. It would transform every social good into a commodity. This is market imperialism."[50] In light of this, Walzer believes, redistribution may be necessary in some cases. These redistributions could take three forms: blocking some trades, taxation, or challenging property rights. "All three redistributions redraw the line between politics and economics, and they do so in ways that strengthen the sphere of politics — the hand of citizens, that is, not necessarily the power of the state."[51] For Walzer, the state must play the crucial role of guardian of the boundaries of the spheres in order to maintain distributive justice.[52] If this role of guardian is expanded too far, however, the state itself can become the boundary-crossing tyrant that must be resisted.

Finally, *equality* serves as the criterion for distribution in other spheres. Equality is always a comparative standard: equality of what, and within which groups? In areas such as political rights, equality is

---

49. "In the marketplace, desert seems to hang on the state of the economy. It can't really be seen independently from a moment in the economy. . . . The market doesn't recognize desert. Initiative, enterprise, innovation, hard work, ruthless dealing, reckless gambling, the prostitution of talent: all these are sometimes rewarded, sometimes not. But the rewards that the market provides, when it provides them, are appropriate to these sorts of effort." *Spheres*, pp. 108-9.
50. *Spheres*, p. 119.
51. *Spheres*, p. 122.
52. *Spheres*, p. 281.

the legitimate standard. Each person who is a citizen has the same rights as do all other citizens. For example, in the political sphere no one gets two votes because they are strong or rich or beautiful, and all citizens have access to the same judicial processes. However, Walzer does not imply that a purely equal distribution of goods constitutes a fair distribution. Rather, in a way that parallels Amartya Sen, he uses the concept of "complex equality" to indicate that equality permits people to be different once their basic civil equalness has been recognized. Walzer calls this "complex equality": each person is unique, and permitting all persons to be uniquely themselves is the goal of complex equality. This may require a different set of goods for some than for others.[53]

David Miller's Appropriation of Walzer

Since its publication in 1983, Walzer's theory of complex equality and spheres of justice has provoked many responses, as well as some clarifications from Walzer himself. The strongest challenge to Walzer's position is the charge of relativism — or of conventionalism. Walzer's critics argue that his system may not guarantee basic rights,[54] and seems to merely recognize established social conventions.[55] In response to such criticisms, Walzer acknowledges:

53. *Spheres*, p. 316.

54. Michael Rustin says: "It is, for example, difficult to find grounds within Walzer's relativist position for intervention to end or mitigate gross social injustices (for example, the oppression of women) where these injustices have not already become the subject of contention within a society." "Equality in Post-Modern Times," in Miller and Walzer, eds., *Pluralism, Justice, and Equality*, p. 31.

55. Brian Barry argues: "His [Walzer's] position would best be described not as relativism at all but as conventionalism: the view that justice (what really is just, not merely what is locally called just) is determined for each society by the shared beliefs of the members of that society about the meanings of the goods that are to be distributed among them." "Spherical Justice and Global Injustice," in Miller and Walzer, p. 75.

We need a theory of human rights (or its functional equivalent in other cultures) to set the basic parameters within which distributions take place. The theory would derive, presumably, from a view of persons rather than of the things they make, and it would establish limits on how these persons may be treated.[56]

Walzer thus seems amenable to a "both/and" approach that would combine a minimal, or "thin," morality, which includes a basic set of human rights, with a "thick" morality, which is particular to each culture. Each person would have a basic set of political and sustenance rights and then would also participate in various spheres of activity in which goods are distributed according to different criteria.

British political philosopher David Miller also levels a charge, though a lesser one. While largely agreeing that goods ought to be distributed according to different norms in different spheres, Miller argues that it is problematical to define a sphere of justice on the basis of the nature of the goods within it. For Miller, "Walzer's approach has a great deal to commend it, but one difficulty it faces is that it seems unable to deal with the case where people seriously and authentically disagree about how justice requires a social good to be allocated."[57] Miller points to education as a possible example of a social good about whose distribution people may legitimately disagree. On what grounds should it be distributed — ability to pay, scholastic aptitude, vocational goals, societal needs, or family ties? Instead of assuming that the nature of the good in question determines the nature of the distribution, Miller proposes that the grounds for determining what constitutes distributive justice in a given sphere be deciding on the basis of the kind of human relationship that characterizes that sphere. For Miller, three basic, ideal kinds of relationships characterize life in society: "solidaristic com-

56. Michael Walzer, "Response," in Miller and Walzer, p. 293.
57. Miller, *Principles of Social Justice* (Cambridge, MA: Harvard University Press, 1999), p. 25.

munities, instrumental associations, and citizenship."[58] Each kind of relationship, then, has its corresponding norm for justice that flows from the character of the relationships occurring within them. Miller agrees with Walzer that the appropriate criteria for distribution within distinct spheres are need, equality, and desert. How does Miller's amendment tighten Walzer's proposal?

Miller defines solidaristic communities as those groups that include people who share a common identity and ethos, such as a family, a club, or a religious group. They are bound together by beliefs, kinship, or culture.[59] Within this kind of social sphere, the defining criterion for distributive justice is that of need.

> Each community embodies, implicitly or explicitly, a sense of the standards that an adequate human life must meet, and it is in terms of this benchmark that the much-contested distinction between needs, which are matters of justice, and mere wants is drawn.[60]

The second way of relating socially is via "instrumental association," in which people engage with each other for a specific purpose, and to achieve a specific goal. "Here people relate to one another in a utilitarian manner; each has aims and purposes that can best be realized by collaboration with others."[61] This kind of association is characteristic of business relationships between buyers and sellers, or between managers and employees. The criterion for distributive justice in these kinds of social relationships is that of desert. The question determining how things should be distributed in these spheres is: how much did person X contribute toward goal Y? Concretely, how much did the field hand earn from the farmer, or the farmer from the grocer? Are you being paid a fair wage, and is your employer getting a fair day's work? Miller says: "Each per-

58. Miller, p. 26.
59. Miller, p. 26.
60. Miller, p. 27.
61. Miller, p. 26.

son comes to the association as a free agent with a set of skills and talents that he deploys to advance its goals. Justice is done when he receives back by way of reward an equivalent to the contribution he makes."[62]

The third kind of social relationship is that of citizenship: "Anyone who is a full member of a society is understood to be the bearer of a set of rights and obligations that together define the status of citizen."[63] Within this sphere, equality is the regulative principle of distributive justice. One citizen cannot be given more or fewer rights than another without undoing the meaning of citizenship. The same laws regarding political participation or trial by jury, for example, must apply to all citizens equally. Miller recognizes that the modes of relating overlap, and that some relationships may be a mixture of two or three kinds of social interaction (he uses marriage as an example). In other cases it may also be that one person may relate to me in more than one way: for example, my grocer, to whom I relate in an economic way in his store, may also be my fellow church member, to whom I might turn in situations of need, and an equal citizen of my country, with whom I might sit on a jury. Each of these relationships with this same person, however, is understood within its particular kind of social interaction, and will thus be regulated by a different criterion of justice. Miller also recognizes that conflicts may sometimes arise among different spheres.[64] He believes that health care, for example, is a service that seems to stand at the border between instrumental association and citizenship. (It seems to me that solidaristic community might also be in play.) For example, should health care be distributed on the basis of whether one can afford a health insurance policy or on the basis of one's equal standing as a citizen, or on the grounds of one's needs as a member of the human family?

Achieving just distribution requires that we match these ideal

62. Miller, p. 28.
63. Miller, p. 30.
64. Miller, p. 35.

types with actual social relationships. What kind of group is this? Is it only one kind, or partly one and partly another? Walzer sees the process of asking and answering these questions as the way that societies give each person his or her due. He says: "Different goods to different companies of men and women for different reasons and in accordance with different procedures. And to get all this right, or to get it roughly right, is to map out the entire social world."[65]

Summary and Synthesis of Kuyper, Walzer, and Miller

Kuyper and Walzer provide a complementary picture of justice using the concept of "spheres." Though Walzer is not dependent on Kuyper, each contributes to the other, permitting us to use their work as a platform for a viable theory of justice. While their works are complementary, there are differences between them, and each has weaknesses that the other strengthens. In Kuyper, for example, the "spheres" can become unwieldy: there seems to be no limit to their number or their types. It is also not clear whether spheres refer to institutions, ways of living, or relationships. Walzer, with Miller's modification, clarifies and shapes Kuyper's dynamic organism into a well-formed structure. For Walzer and Miller, there are not innumerable spheres; there are only three distinct kinds of spheres, and they correspond to the three basic kinds of human relationships: instrumental, solidaristic, and citizenship. Each of these spheres is in turn regulated by a single principle of justice, respectively, desert, need, and equality. This condensation and clarification permits us to identify where particular norms of justice are appropriate. Kuyper's concepts alone would not make that possible.

Kuyper also fills in a possible gap in Walzer's presentation. In *Spheres,* Walzer's proposal does not specifically address the nature of the state and its relationship to the individual. With Kuyper, we get a plausible worldview that includes the state as well as the spheres.

65. Walzer, *Spheres*, p. 26.

Kuyper's viewpoint permits us to escape the either/or of state totalitarianism, which claims that all institutions are authorized and derived from the state (state sovereignty), on the one hand, and an individualism that claims that all institutions are merely the composites of the wills of individuals (popular sovereignty), on the other hand. Thanks to Kuyper, we can recognize the legitimacy of the various spheres and the institutions in their own right, deriving authority from God the Creator. Walzer's theory, without this support, seems to depend on the nature of the goods themselves, with little consideration of the nature and kinds of human institutions that direct their distribution.

For Walzer, a basic set of rights apart from those that arise from the nature of the goods distributed is also problematical. His critics took up this charge, and he admitted its legitimacy: "We need a theory of human rights . . . to set the basic parameters within which distributions take place. The theory would derive, presumably, from a view of persons rather than of the things they make, and it would establish limits on how these persons may be treated."[66] Kuyper's theologically based system addresses this weakness: in Kuyper we find a view of persons as precious God-imagers who are uniquely responsible and creative.[67] This anthropology, derived from the Christian tradition, would set the basic rights parameters that establish limits as to how we may treat one another. It would also permit us to ground

---

66. Walzer, "Response," p. 293. My reading of Walzer suggests there may be a gap in his anthropology. It seems that he may not have sufficiently developed a "view of persons" (anthropology) that would in fact make it possible for his system to carry such a set of basic rights. Oddly, this gap does not seem to be addressed by the critical work on Walzer. A recent critical study of Walzer, Michael Haus's *Die Politische Philosophie Michael Walzer*, for example, only speaks of Walzer's view of humanity in relation to particular contexts, but does not raise questions of the "nature" of humankind (see especially the section on "Gemeinsames Leben und individuelle Zustimmung," pp. 122-27).

67. While I did not speak earlier of Kuyper's own anthropological views in this chapter, his writings and his theological tradition certainly affirm a view of creation and creature that are consistent with the "image of God" language used in Chapter Four.

our understanding of "solidaristic communities" in strong theological terrain. Given an anthropology that assumes that all of humankind has the same nature, and that each is his "brother's keeper," Christian theology extends the sphere of solidaristic community as far as the whole human family.

All humans are, in fact, part of one basic solidaristic group on the basis of our unity as fellow children and image-bearers of God: we share one human nature, one divinely inspired purpose, and one divinely created world. In the parable of the Good Samaritan, Jesus demonstrated how love for others, which sums up the law, is in evidence when one neighbor serves another who is in need. The Samaritan was thus the true law-keeper, neighbor, and friend. As members of one familial group, we owe one another those basic material things that people need to be able to function as full humans in God's world. If we deny that those on the neediest margins of society are worthy of this, we are denying that all people are really part of one race, one family, and one created people. This would be to say that the needs of others do not count because they live on a distant continent, or because their skin is a different color, or because they behave in strange ways. Failing to provide basic sustenance implies that their claims have no merit. Such arguments would deny either the claimants' solidarity in the human race or the legitimacy of their claim to the basic sustenance required to live as God's children in God's world.

I acknowledge that there may be a range of responsibility among members of solidaristic groups, as there are in the other spheres. Thus I do not believe that I am equally responsible to all the people in the basic solidaristic group that we call humanity. For example, in an instrumental group such as a club, my responsibilities may only include sending in an absentee ballot and paying some dues, whereas being a citizen of a nation may require that I serve in its military and pay with my life. Or, if I am the CEO of a corporation, my responsibility for achieving its goals is far greater than that of its part-time cleaning service worker. So, too, in solidaristic relationships. For example, as a parent of children, I am morally responsible to care for and protect them at great risk and cost, perhaps to the point of complete self-sacrifice. Thus, my degree of responsibility for humans seems to vary according to the depth of my relationship to them. However, I question whether the fact that I am a citizen of one nation removes or even lessens my responsibility to provide basic needs to someone in another nation.[68] And the fact that my responsibility may be lesser or secondary in some cases does not mean that there is no responsibility at all. In keeping with the biblical mandate, a base line for our responsibility to other humans is that we provide each other with basic sustenance. When these basic needs of the human family are met, true justice will be found.

This proposal for distributive justice derives from the conceptualizations of Michael Walzer in *Spheres of Justice* and David Miller in *Principles of Social Justice*. While I agree that the proposal for distributive justice provided by these contemporary political theorists is indeed strong, their proposal can be strengthened if we incorporate Christian theology into them — in four significant ways.

First, using Kuyper and the Christian theology he espoused allows us to ground our anthropology in a more substantive way than do Walzer and Miller. Using a biblical starting point, we have been able to begin with human beings as created in the image and likeness of God. This combination of physical and spiritual nature as part of the image of God provides us with grounds for honoring the claim to basic sustenance, since sustenance is necessary to live as a God-imager. We have further come to see that our human nature as re-creators entails that we must have the opportunity to continue God's own creative work. Finally, we have observed that our nature as God's representatives entails responsibility for the care and development of creation. This theological starting point permits us to address the basic questions underlying issues of distributive justice. For

---

68. The notion that the nearness of our relationships determines the degree of responsibility toward that person goes back at least as far as St. Augustine. However, Peter Singer, in *One World: The Ethics of Globalization* (New Haven: Yale University Press, 2002), argues that national boundaries should not affect our responsibility for others. The parable of the Good Samaritan also seems to challenge a view based on our conventional definition of "neighbor."

example: Who is the being that merits what she needs? Why is it that creatures called "human" are so worthy of respect? Why are humans responsible for each other? Christian faith affirms that all humans are inestimably valuable: each derives her or his nature from God, each is a child for whom the Son of God died, and each is a person with whom God desires to live. Because humans are innately and immeasurably precious and "God-like," doing them justice is treating them as the bearers of God's image, as we should.

Second, a theological starting point for distributive justice also guarantees that no temporal, human, or earthly sphere can become the absolute norm or good, or the final point of reference for all the others, since the final norm and good is God alone. The beginning and end points for this perspective on justice are thus transcendent. Ultimately, the good of each sphere is derived from the good of the One who is beyond them. No sphere — or aspect of it — may become absolute; to permit this would be idolatrous.

Third, and conversely, the fact that the spheres are set in place by God grants them an origin and status apart from church or state or individual. Spheres such as business or family or sports are valid and independent — apart from their relationship to church or state or individual. From the Kuyperian perspective, other spheres are not authorized by the church, nor by the state, nor by the popular will. Only God authorizes them.

Finally, on the basis of this faith-based starting point, we can legitimately prioritize the right to basic sustenance over secondary rights.[69] I wish to honor this claim based on need as a basic moral right. Other claims, such as those based on contribution or desert, are secondary. Seeking to honor the right to basic sustenance, I have tried to show that "business as usual" in the marketplace may yield commutative justice for some — in which, for example, salaries are fair for some — but it will not yield basic sustenance for all.

69. This prioritization in rights is apparent in the writings of Henry Shue. He refers to these two kinds of rights as being part of "basic rights" (cited in Chapter Five).

Using Kuyper, Walzer, and Miller, I propose the following definition of distributive justice: A state of just distribution occurs when all members of humanity receive their basic needs, when citizens receive equal treatment, and when producers receive proportional reward on the basis of their contribution. This proposal for distributive justice challenges current priorities, and I will show how such challenges can be met in practice in the final chapter.

CHAPTER SEVEN

What We Can Really Accomplish

"Heavenly Father, forgive us for sins of omission, as well as those of commission."

Paul Van Til's evening prayers

The underlying problem that motivates this book is that tens of millions of people like my friend Ester still lack basic sustenance. The *Human Development Report, 2005,* compares poverty to the tsunami that struck Indonesia in 2005. The tsunami was a highly visible, unpredictable, and largely unpreventable tragedy. Other tragedies are less visible, monotonously predictable and readily preventable. Every hour more than 1,200 children die, but they do so away from the glare of media attention. That's the equivalent of three tsunamis a month, every month, directed exclusively at the world's most vulnerable citizens — its children. The causes of death will vary, but the overwhelming majority can be traced to a single pathology: poverty.[1]

In light of this situation and the Christian claim that all people merit basic sustenance, I have advanced a proposal for distributive

---

1. *Human Development Report, 2005.* New York: United Nations Development Program, p. 1.

justice in the previous chapter that could guide us toward a remedy. This proposal, derived from Kuyper, Walzer, and Miller, argues that we must validate claims to goods based on need, not just achievement and equality. *A state of just distribution will occur when all members of the human race have their basic needs met, when citizens receive equal treatment, and when producers receive rewards in proportion to their contribution.*[2] I believe that this proposal both complements and challenges a free-market approach to distribution. In this chapter I will show that at least three economic traditions are capable of incorporating the claim to basic needs within a market system. I will then address some objections that might arise. Finally, I wish to recommend the kind of action that will provide basic sustenance for all. As I do so, I hope to show that the provision of basic sustenance for all is not a utopian dream but a realizable task.

We cannot assume that the free market will provide basic sustenance for all. The problem with the free market alone is that goods are distributed only on one basis — desert. You get what you earn, or you get what you can pay for. The free market does not address claims based on need. In the market, a person's marginal contribution to market productivity is the sole reason she or he has an effective claim to goods and services. A hungry child, however, can claim nothing from the market. She must come up with the effective demand — money — to pay for any item of food.

Given this critique, one might assume that I oppose distribution of goods via free-market exchange. I do not. In fact, I believe that most goods *should* be exchanged via the free market, because it is an extraordinarily effective means of distribution, and it promotes commutative justice within the economic sphere. It rewards those who contribute economically, and sometimes it punishes those who will not contribute. It provides tremendous freedoms within which individuals can choose how they use their resources. It does not *compel*

---

2. I recognize that, even if just distribution were to occur, other kinds of justice might still be elusive. For example, racism, militarism, and sexual violence would not be rooted out even in a state of affairs described above. My focus has been "distributive justice." I take the issues just mentioned to be part of a larger "social justice."

anyone to make evil purchases; it *permits* everyone to make good purchases. What's more, there is simply no better system for distributing goods available. Peoples and societies have tried various forms of socialism, communism, and egalitarianism, and they have failed. Replacing an effective market with an ineffective command system has been historically shown to cause greater harm than good. Therefore, I acknowledge — and even celebrate — the good and the justice that the market provides at this point.

While I agree that the market standard of desert based on economic contribution is appropriate in "instrumental" spheres such as business, that is not to say that the justice of the marketplace is sufficient.[3] As we have discovered, it does not provide basic sustenance for all God's children. As a result, a system of distributive justice that uses *only* the free market is necessarily less comprehensive and less just than one that also recognizes the validity of claims based on need.

Promising Economic Directions

At least three schools of economics explicitly endorse claims based on need, as well as equality and desert, and I have relied on all of them at various points in this book. Each of them holds promise for implementing a system for distributive justice that recognizes claims based on need: Amartya Sen and the concept of "basic capabilities," the Kuyperian tradition, and social economics.[4] In different ways,

3. Recall from Chapter Six that David Miller defines instrumental relationships and the justice within them in this way: "Here [in instrumental relationships] people relate to one another in a utilitarian manner; each has aims and purposes that can best be realized by collaboration with others." Miller, *Principles of Social Justice*, p. 27. "Justice is done when he receives back by way of reward an equivalent to the contribution he makes." Miller, p. 28.

4. While it may be the case that the "socio-economics" of Etzioni et al., is compatible with this perspective, I limit myself here to social economists affiliated with the *International Journal of Social Economics*.

and to differing degrees, each of these economic schools accommodates all three aspects of distributive justice proposed: the negative political rights that protect property and life, the right to basic sustenance for all, and commutative rights. Since I earlier described Amartya Sen's proposal that people must possess the capabilities necessary for basic functioning, I will not rehearse it here. However, I do wish to highlight the fact that Sen prioritizes human need in his creative theory, using the "capacity to function" as his criterion. I will now briefly describe the other two economic "schools" that can help us go forward to meet the unaddressed issue of need in mainstream economics.

Economists within the Kuyperian tradition have developed possible options that recognize the genuine but limited good of market exchange, but also support need as a legitimate criterion for distribution. For a sketch of how this economic school might help promote the kinds of justice we seek, I turn to two contemporary economists within this tradition, Bob Goudzwaard and John Tiemstra. Tiemstra does not begin his economic theorizing with the mainstream view of the rational individual who seeks to satisfy preferences efficiently. Instead, he addresses the normative issues of distribution from the start:

> Any approach which does not from the beginning consider what the relations of wealth and income among various groups and contributors should be — that is, a normative approach — misconceives what actually happens. Moreover, it is not difficult to show that the various views of what is fair do, in fact, structure particular distributional arrangements, so that it is only with a normative distributional framework that the actual situation in a modern economy can be properly addressed.[5]

---

5. John Tiemstra, *Reforming Economics*, Toronto Studies in Theology, vol. 48 (Lewiston, NY: The Edwin Mellen Press, 1990), p. 26.

In order to shape desired economic outcomes, Tiemstra proposes that economists first picture the kind of society and the kinds of people we wish to create, and then decide which policies will likely achieve them. Tiemstra describes this relationship between society and economics in which the former clearly defines and directs the latter:

> A proper view of economics involves a proper view of all of life. Economic considerations form just one of the aspects of life, part of humanity's existence before God, and the significance of economic aspects of life must not and cannot be considered apart from the meaning of life itself.[6]

The desired distributional outcome in Tiemstra's economics, for example, would not necessarily be a Pareto optimal condition, as it is in mainstream economics. Rather, it would be a state of affairs in which the basic needs of all are met, so that each person can be a potential participant in human society. Unlike in mainstream theory, the desired outcome does not derive from an aggregation of individual preference satisfactions but from a view of human society as a complex set of social interrelationships. Following Kuyper, these economists see each sphere of life as unique, requiring different criteria for justice within each.

Kuyperian economists also acknowledge that free trade and exchange is fitting and just within its proper sphere. Bob Goudzwaard,[7] for example, praises free trade, and speaks appreciatively of the global marketplace:

> The principle of sphere sovereignty welcomes economic and technological development and sees them as an inalienable as-

6. Tiemstra, p. 63.

7. See Bob Goudzwaard and Harry DeLange, *Beyond Poverty and Affluence* (Grand Rapids: Eerdmans, 1995); Bob Goudzwaard, *Capitalism and Progress* (Toronto: Wedge Publications, 1979); *Aid for the Overdeveloped West* (Toronto: Wedge Publications, 1975), as well as numerous articles.

pect of our calling in God's creation. There is nothing in this reformational principle that forbids the economy and technology from gradually acquiring global characteristics.[8]

Goudzwaard views the market as an effective tool that can be used to serve both God and neighbor. He claims: "One of the most important elements of a Christian economic policy is . . . to appeal to people to moderate their pursuit of prosperity and direct their spending to God's honour and the service of the neighbour."[9]

Tiemstra, from his perspective, which sees economic activity as a means of service, proposes an important redefinition of the task of economics: "Economics, on our view, is the study of the communal stewardship and organization of the creation to meet human needs."[10] This "stewardship" implies management of resources in such a way as to create the kind of society that permits all people to participate.

Tiemstra has here chosen a clear alternative to mainstream theory. It is remarkable inasmuch as it prioritizes the provision of basic needs as the first task of economics (and perhaps minimizes exchange too much). Whereas mainstream theory rewards productivity and virtually ignores needs, Tiemstra's definition of economics demotes claims based on *desert* and promotes those based on *need*. He also appears to treat the provision of basic needs as a primary right.

A third economic tradition that supports the claim to basic sustenance for all — social economics — has a long historical trajectory in Europe[11] and includes contemporary American economists such as

---

8. Bob Goudzwaard, "Globalization, Regionalization, and Sphere Sovereignty," in Luis E. Lugo, ed., *Religion, Pluralism, and Public Life: Abraham Kuyper's Legacy for the Twenty-First Century* (Grand Rapids: Eerdmans, 2000), p. 335.

9. Cited from the platform of the Reformed Political Alliance, a Dutch political party, in Van Haeften, et al., *Wegen naar werk,* Groen van Prinsterer Stichting (Gronigen: De Vuurbaak, 1979), p. 68 (translated by John Boersema as *Political-Economic Activity to the Honour of God* [Winnipeg: Premier Publishing, 1999], p. 85).

10. Tiemstra, p. 66.

11. See Thomas O. Nitsch, "Social Economics: From Search for Identity to Quest

John B. Davis, Mark A. Lutz, and Edward O'Boyle.[12] One character-istic of this long line of thinkers is a refusal to separate normative from positive economics. One economist in this tradition even de-fines social economics as "a *moral* science of what ought to be and must be done."[13] Defining itself in terms of Adam Smith's older "po-litical economy" rather than as a contemporary positive science, the social economics school sees itself as one perspective on the social or-der that recognizes as falling within its purview not only those things measured in monetary exchange but also other social factors that contribute to human well-being. William M. Dugger presents five characteristics of social economics:

1. It is a value-directed approach to solving the problems of the dis-advantaged.
2. Amelioration rather than preservation or revolution is its aim.
3. Social economists are impelled to be activists, within the limita-tions of their own life-situations.
4. Understanding is sought through a holistic rather than a reduc-tionistic approach.
5. Society, the fabric within which the strands of problems are wo-ven, is viewed as an organic whole.[14]

Each of these characteristics stands in contrast to mainstream economic theory. First, by insisting that economics is value-directed, social economics denies the claim that economists treat only positive facts, while deriving values from elsewhere. Thus it addresses values

---

for Roots; or, Social Economics: The First 100 Years," in *The International Journal of Social Economics* 14, nos. 3-5: 70-87.

12. Davis, Lutz, and O'Boyle self-identify as social economists and are associated with the *Review of Social Economy*. Others who do not so self-identify but share some characteristics of social economics include Robert Heilbroner and Daniel Hausman, cited at various times above.

13. Nitsch, p. 81.

14. William M. Dugger, "Social Economics: One Perspective," *Review of Social Economy* 35, no. 3 (Dec. 1977): 300.

such as provision for all in its economic theorizing. Second, it does not see either the "preservation" of the status quo of property ownership often found in capitalism or the "revolution" of Marxism as satisfactory options. Instead, social economists opt for the "amelioration" of poverty and the growth of equality. Third, social economists also attempt to practice what they preach: they do not want to divorce their professional commitments from their human commitments while, for example, speaking "only as economists." Fourth, they propose a holistic approach to poverty that addresses it as a many-faceted social problem rather than as a narrowly defined economic problem. Finally, social economists, too, view society as an organic whole, seeing it not as merely the aggregate of its individuals but as a complex organism.[15]

Clearly, social economics promotes theory and practice that fits the proposal for distributive justice derived from Kuyper, Walzer, and Miller. It recognizes that values are inherent in economics, and consciously seeks to promote greater equality. It seeks to eliminate poverty through broad-based social programs. It also recognizes the legitimacy of market freedoms and rights.

Although the formulations and perhaps certain underlying philosophical assumptions of Amartya Sen, the "social economics" school, and the Kuyperian tradition may differ,[16] these schools share a number of important characteristics that make them supportive of this proposal for distributive justice. All three recognize that: (1) the "rational choice" theory of mainstream economics is not sufficient to explain all of human behavior; (2) there is an important and legitimate role for free exchange and entrepreneurial development; (3) a just distribution of material goods will require that we prioritize the basic human need for sustenance; (4) society and society's well-being is not merely an aggregate of each individual's satisfactions; but they all form part of an organic whole; and (5) Pareto optimality is inadequate

15. Dugger, pp. 300-310.

16. For example, the Kuyperians are overtly Christian in their anthropological assumptions, whereas the other two schools may possess a variety of anthropological viewpoints.

to describe true human well-being. I believe that all of these rivulets from outside of the mainstream are refreshing sources that support my picture of distributive justice.

Objections

Some may object that redistribution is, of necessity, wrong. Evangelical theologian Calvin Beisner, for example, argues that any system of justice that shows partiality to some individuals, even the poor, is incompatible with the true standard of justice, which of necessity is impartial.[17] For Beisner, "all other regulations of economic activity other than those necessary to prohibit, prevent, and punish fraud, theft and violence are therefore unjust."[18] Beisner and other libertarians have a very firm notion of the inherent justice of the status quo: initial endowments are sacred, as are the property rights that protect them. In fact, these rights take priority over human claims based on need.

I see at least three flaws here. First, from a Christian viewpoint, the Bible does in fact show partiality for the widow, the orphan, and the alien, and the grounds for this "preferential option" is, very simply, their neediness. The Bible also clearly shows that property is held in trust. In Leviticus 25:23, God says, "The land is mine; with me you are but aliens and tenants" (NRSV). God holds the mortgage on all our property and requires that it be used in service of the community — especially the needy within the community. In Deuteronomy 10:17-18, God declares himself to be impartial in judgment and the defender of the widow and the orphan: "For the LORD your God is God of gods and Lord of lords, the great, mighty, and terrible God.

17. E. Calvin Beisner, "Justice and Poverty: Two Views Contrasted," in Herbert Schlossberg, Vinay Samuel, and Ronald J. Sider, eds., *Christianity and Economics in the Post Cold-War Era — The Oxford Declaration and Beyond* (Grand Rapids: Eerdmans, 1994), p. 58.

18. E. Calvin Beisner, *Prosperity and Poverty: The Compassionate Use of Resources in a World of Scarcity* (Westchester, IL: Crossway Books, 1988), p. 54.

He is no respecter of persons; he is not to be bribed; he secures justice for the fatherless and the widow, and he shows love towards the alien who lives among you, giving him food and clothing."

Second, the notion of "distribution" versus "redistribution" is a fiction. There is no pristine state of distribution from which all other arrangements are unjust redistributions. Goods are always flowing. Where would our original state of "distribution" begin? Would it begin before our European ancestors took the land from the North American Indians? Would it begin before the egregious accounting scandals at Enron that left thousands without pensions? Would it begin before or after various corporations were chartered and patents were issued? Would it begin before we were born in the United States and Ester was born in Central America? Clearly, there is no such thing as an initial distribution point from which changes are to be regarded as unjust, inasmuch as they are *re*distribution. This is an ahistorical position that serves as a justification of a status quo that leaves millions without basic necessities.

In addition to ignoring history, the argument against any form of redistribution ignores the reality of power. The libertarian position advocates that we simply follow the rules of the game, assuming that the rules are agreed upon. Consider the following as an example of the kind of game that might result. The rules of baseball are well-established: each team gets three outs, there are three strikes and four balls possible in each at-bat, you must tag up on fly balls, and so forth. All baseball teams throughout the world agree on these rules. Let's say that the New York Yankees agree to play my church's team, the Brookfield Reformers, and agree to honor all the rules when the game is played. Is that a "fair" ballgame? The libertarian may have to answer yes: that is, if the rules are agreed upon and followed, the results — inevitable though they may be — are "fair." Most people — and I include myself among them — would question not only whether this was a fair ballgame but whether it was a baseball game at all. The discrepancies in power and skill are so great that what happens on the field might be considered a kind of circus — or a form of humiliation. We could go even further. Let's say that the

Yankees agree that they will be permitted only two strikes per at-bat and two outs per inning. In other words, the rules are now unfairly biased against them. Even though my friend Rob Buikema, a 49-year-old labor attorney, is a good shortstop, would anyone bet on him batting or fielding better than Derek Jeter? Would anyone care to bet on the Brookfield Reformers winning this game that is now grossly "unfair" in their favor? Enough! Following the rules will not necessarily create justice.

Someone else may object that, while helping the needy is certainly a laudable thing, doing so is an act of mercy or love, but not justice. Again, I believe that the Bible speaks against that notion. The Bible makes commands: leave the gleanings in the field, declare a Year of Jubilee, redeem the property of your brother, do not hold back the wages of a hired hand, be open-handed toward any of your countrymen who are in poverty and need, and so forth. All of these are, very simply, *commands*. Not one of them is found in a biblical appendix labeled "For the Especially Merciful." Furthermore, this objection is based on a false distinction between love and law. Jesus says, "If you love me, you will keep my commandments," and "if you keep my commandments, you will abide in my love" (John 14:15; 15:10, NRSV). Law and love are not at opposite poles to each other in Scripture; they support each other. The International Standard Bible Encyclopedia reference on "justice" puts it well:

> The major point is that God's justice is no abstraction at odds with an equally abstract mercy. To the contrary, as the description "a righteous God and a Savior" implies (Isa. 45:21), God's justice seeks concretely to express His mercy and to accomplish His salvation (Jgs. 5:11; Ps. 7:17; 35:23f.; 51:14; 71:15; 103:17; Isa. 46:13; 51:5f.). . . . By these requirements ["To do justice, and to love kindness, and to walk humbly with your God" (Mic. 6:8)] God's goodness is structured into the social order.[19]

19. J. G. Gibbs, "Just," in *The International Standard Bible Encyclopedia* (Grand Rapids: Eerdmans, 1982), II, p. 1167.

Nowhere does Scripture support an opposition between love and justice that leaves the provision of basic sustenance as an optional claim. This false distinction between mercy and justice in Scripture also leads to a false distinction between civil and religious law: that is, civil laws are enforceable, and the religious laws are unenforceable and optional. Related to this is the objection that providing basic sustenance for all is not a task that the government should coerce but one that people of good will should freely take up. While I agree that it is a task that people of good will should certainly take up, it is also a matter of justice, and government can rightfully coerce it.

First of all, it is clear that the government does have the authority to coerce. It coerces me to pay taxes, to drive responsibly, to support public education, and so forth. It even coerces me to help finance things that many believe are evil — such as fighting unprovoked wars, aborting unborn children, and building anti-ballistic missile systems that don't work. How much more can the government coerce a good, such as the provision of basic needs for all?

Second, the government *can* rightfully coerce us to provide basic sustenance for all as a matter of justice. Nicholas Wolterstorff argues this point well:

> I want to say, as emphatically as I can, that our concern with poverty is not an issue of generosity but of rights. If a rich man knows of someone who is starving and has the power to help that person but chooses not to do so, then he violates the starving person's rights as surely and reprehensibly as if he had physically assaulted the sufferer.[20]

While I am not certain that the rights are violated *as* reprehensibly as in a physical assault, the point is taken. Harm is done to the weak, be it by omission or commission. Rights are indeed violated, and rights

20. Wolterstorff, *Until Justice and Peace Embrace* (Grand Rapids: Eerdmans), p. 82.

and justice are matters of state. Yes, the government is capable of acting and justified in acting, and it should act.

Poverty and Development

While a theory of distributive justice may well offer a way forward in addressing the problem of basic human needs, the outstanding problem for activating such a proposal is clearly moral and political. In most contemporary societies, the claim to basic sustenance is either not recognized as a political right at all, or it is seen only as a moral option.[21] While many programs throughout the world do relieve deprivation,[22] the claim to basic sustenance has not been validated by a political body capable of enforcing it. The moral right to basic sustenance is thus a political orphan. Pressing the claim for public validation of the right to basic sustenance is an outstanding challenge of our time. Thus far, the many noble statements that address this issue are not enforceable, and thus they leave basic needs unmet.

Which governmental policies shall be pursued to provide to those lacking basic sustenance? Exactly how shall goods be distributed, and who shall distribute them? I cannot pretend to answer a host of such policy questions. As I have noted earlier, strategies for the provision of basic sustenance could include a range of policies designed to "avoid deprivation, protect persons from deprivation, and aid the deprived."[23] Since the answer to such policy questions changes from place to place and time to time, the means of meeting the proposed

21. As noted earlier, the *United Nations Declaration of Human Rights* does not bear the force of law, especially Articles 23, 24, and 25, which treat economic rights. See Ian Brownlie, ed., *Basic Documents on Human Rights* (Oxford: Clarendon Press, 1992), pp. 25-26.

22. Some societies (Scandinavian countries come to mind) do in effect provide basic sustenance for all of their citizens via a network of social programs. The further issue, which I will not address here, is how national borders affect one's responsibility to meet the needs of basic sustenance.

23. Henry Shue, *Basic Rights: Subsistence, Affluence and U.S. Foreign Policy* (Princeton: Princeton University Press, 1980), pp. 52-53.

norms of justice will also change over time and place. Wise economists, politicians, businesspeople, citizens, and believers together, in
their particular contexts, must answer these policy questions in the
push and pull of local, national, and international governance.

I wish to conclude, however, with some data showing that alleviation of much of the world's greatest needs is in fact a real possibility.
Many Americans think that "foreign aid" is now solving much of the
problem of poverty. Philosopher Peter Singer notes: "Two surveys
show that U.S. citizens assume that foreign aid accounts for between
15 and 20% of government spending, and would like to cut that
amount to between 5 and 10%."[24] But the reality is that foreign aid
stands at approximately 0.10 percent of the United States' gross national product (GNP). Singer continues:

> And even this miserly sum exaggerates the U.S. aid to the most
> needy, for much of it is strategically targeted for political pur-
> poses. The largest single recipient of U.S. official development
> assistance is Egypt. (Russia and Israel get even more aid from
> the United States than Egypt, but it is not classified as develop-
> ment assistance.) Tiny Bosnia and Herzegovina gets a larger
> allocation from the United States than India.[25]

Some may quickly point out that, in addition to official government aid, the citizens of the United States also contribute privately to
many charities that provide aid. This is true. But Singer responds,
once again, with disturbing facts:

> Non-government aid . . . amounts to $4 billion, or about 40
> percent of government aid. So adding in the non-government
> aid takes the United States aid total only from 0.10 percent to
> 0.14 percent of GNP. . . . Compare this 14 billion to the annual

24. Singer, *One World: The Ethics of Globalization* (New Haven: Yale University Press, 2004), p. 183.
25. Singer, p. 181.

spending on alcohol of $34 billion, or on non-alcoholic beverages of $26 billion.[26]

The bottom line is that, compared to the other developed countries in terms of percentage of GNP, the amount of foreign aid given by the United States ranks dead last.[27]

Nevertheless, the right to basic sustenance can be met. The world economy has more than enough resources to provide basic sustenance for all.[28] In a study of this issue, the Brandt Report says:

> The actual cost for eliminating world poverty is far lower than most people realize. In the late 1990s, the UNDP (United Nations Development Program) projected some of the annual expenses of a global anti-poverty program, including $9 billion for water and sanitation, $6 billion for education, and $13 billion for health and nutrition. According to other estimates from the World Bank, the price tag on a comprehensive international relief package would be about $80 billion a year — about 10% of the world's annual military budget.[29]

In more individualized terms, UNICEF says that a donation of $17 will provide immunization "to protect a child for life against the six leading child-killing and maiming diseases: measles, polio, diphtheria, whooping cough, tetanus, and tuberculosis. . . ."[30] An executive at a Christian development agency told me that, for approximately $200 per year, that agency could "Free a Family" from destitution

---

26. Singer, p. 181.

27. Singer, p. 180.

28. This is not to say that the earth could sustain a situation in which everyone lived at the standard of middle-class North America. I suggest, rather, that there are enough resources — grains, potable water, material for building structures, etc. — to meet the basic needs of the world's population.

29. See the website at www.brandt21forum.info/1cbPoverty.html. I am grateful to my friend Kurt VerBeek for this reference.

30. Singer, p. 187.

and provide it with basic sustenance.[31] The disturbing question is this: Why haven't we each paid the $200? Or, if we have been privileged with opportunity and wealth, why haven't we paid a multiple of the $200?

One reason may be that we have thought foreign aid and charity were doing the job. As we have seen above, they are not. Another reason may be that we don't believe that redistributing money is an effective approach to solving the problem. In particular, there may be some countries where the infrastructure is such that more money may only exacerbate the problems. But Joseph Stiglitz, winner of the Nobel Prize and the chief economist of the World Bank, says the following on that subject: "Just as aid is poised to be its most effective, the volume of aid is declining and is at its lowest level ever."[32] In point of fact, a large number of extraordinary people do relief and development work. Among my acquaintances are entrepreneurs who scour Haiti looking for ways to start businesses, agriculturalists who travel the world looking for ways to improve farms, and community developers from "two-thirds world" nations who build up the social base of some of the poorest communities on earth. These farmers, businesspeople, and community development workers can and do get the job done. And more of them, with more resources, could do a great deal more.

Another reason we may not yet have committed our support is that we don't see the reality of starvation and disease and famine close at hand. Few people I know would send a starving child away if he or she showed up on their front doorstep. But the child in Africa, Asia, or Latin America does not receive the generosity from our hands. Does distance really remove responsibility? Philosopher Peter Unger tells this story to illustrate the moral position we may be in:

---

31. Tom Post, of the Christian Reformed World Relief Committee, in conversation with the author, January 2005.

32. Singer, p. 190.

Bob had purchased a vintage sports car but not yet insured it. When driving it home, the car stalled on a railroad track. Leaving his car to get help, he noticed a child stuck on another railroad track that formed a Y with the track his car was on. He walked up the track well past the Y. Meanwhile a runaway train came down the track. There was a switch near him that could send the train either toward his car, or toward the child. One or the other would be destroyed. Bob threw the switch and saved his car.[33]

Most people would find Bob's action morally reprehensible: he chose to save a piece of tin rather than a human life. But in what significant way is Bob's choice different from our own? We know that many are dying, we have the means to save them, and yet we choose to spend our resources on luxuries.

One rationalization may be this: we assume that there were actually a dozen Y's in the track, and that a dozen other people could have thrown the switch, wrecked their car, and saved the child before we did. In a sense, this may be the case. There are others who may be closer, or have more direct knowledge of the child. But if all twelve ahead of us have failed to pull the switch, does the thirteenth not have any responsibility? Or we may be looking at each other and saying, "You can afford to contribute far better than I can." These kinds of rationalizations may well be what lie behind our inaction.

In fact, few of us would be asked to sacrifice something that is as valuable as a vintage sports car. At the Millennium Summit in 2000, the World Bank estimated that it would cost between $40 and $60 billion per year in additional aid to cut poverty in half by 2015. There are approximately 600 million adults in the developed nations of the world. Thus a donation or tax of $100 per year per adult would be on the high side of the estimate of funds needed to cut poverty by half. Eliminating it entirely would certainly be desirable, but half

33. Summary of Peter Unger, *Living High and Letting Die: Our Illusion of Innocence* (New York: Oxford University Press, 1996), pp. 136-39.

would be an enormous blessing. As the ancient Jewish rabbis said, "Whoever destroys a single soul should be considered the same as one who has destroyed a whole world. And whoever saves one single soul is to be considered the same as one who has saved a whole world."[34]

The problem, I repeat, is not a technical one. We have gifted farmers, development workers, teachers, businesspeople, and engineers who already know how to effectively improve human welfare. Nor would a gift or tax of $100-200 per year per person require an overthrow of free-market exchange. Political theorist Charles Lindblom says: "Neither logic nor empirical evidence shows the impossibility — even the improbability — of reconciling a real-world market system with a greatly more egalitarian distribution of wealth and income."[35] The problem is, in fact, a moral one: we have simply not chosen to distribute goods in such a way that the basic needs of all human beings are met.

34. Quoted in Abraham Heschel, *The Prophets* (New York: Harper Torchbooks), vol. 1, p. 14.

35. Charles E. Lindblom, *Politics and Markets: The World's Political-Economic Systems* (New York: Basic Books, 1977), p. 43.

Bibliography

Abrecht, Paul. "From Oxford to Vancouver: Lessons from Fifty Years of Ecumenical Work for Economic and Social Justice." *Ecumenical Review* 40 (Apr. 1988): 147-68.

Alexander, S. "Human Values and Economists' Values." In S. Hook, *Human Values and Economic Policy: A Symposium*. New York: New York University Press, 1967: 101-16.

Anderson, Elizabeth S. "What Is the Point of Equality?" *Ethics* 109 (Jan. 1999): 287-337.

Arendt, Hannah. *The Human Condition*. Chicago: University of Chicago Press, 1958.

Arrow, K. *Social Choice and Individual Values*. New Haven: Yale University Press, 1951.

de Avila, Fernando Bastos, et al. "Modelos de nueva sociedad y etica para un Nuevo orden economico." *Documento CELAM*, 81. Bogotá: Consejo Episcopal Latinoamericano, 1987.

Barrera, Albino. "From Obligations to Rights: Economic Progress and the Language of Ethical Discourse." *Downside Review* 117 (Jan. 1999): 41-58.

Bartell, Ernest. "The United States and Third World Poor in the World Economy: Some Economic and Ethical Issues." In *Catholic Social Teaching and the United States Economy*. Washington: University Press of America, 1984: 259-84.

Bastiat, Frederic. *The Law: The Classic Blueprint for a Just Society*. Trans. Dean Russell. New York: The Foundation for Economic Education, 1998.

Baum, Gregory. "An Ethical Critique of Capitalism: Contributions of Modern Catholic Social Teaching." In *Religion and Economic Justice.* Philadelphia: Temple University Press, 1991: 78-94.

Bellah, Robert N. "Taming the Savage Market." *Christian Century* 108 (Sept. 18-25, 1991): 844-49.

Belshaw, Deryk. "Socio-economic Theology and Ethical Choices in Contemporary Development Policy: An Outline of Biblical Approaches to Social Justice and Poverty Alleviation." *Transformation* 14 (Jan.-Mar. 1997): 5-9.

Benju, Sibusiso. "The 'Root' Causes of Socio-economic and Political Injustice As They Relate to the Development." In *All Africa Lutheran Consultation of Christian Theology and Strategy for Mission.* Geneva: Lutheran World Federation Department of Church Cooperation, 1980: 144-52.

Beversluis, Eric. "A Critique of Ronald Nash on Economic Justice and the State." *Christian Scholar's Review* 11, no. 4 (1982): 330-46.

Block, Walter, and Donald Shaw, eds. *Theology, Third World Development, and Economic Justice.* Vancouver: Fraser Institute, 1985.

Blomberg, Craig L. *Neither Poverty nor Riches: A Biblical Theology of Material Possessions.* Grand Rapids: Eerdmans, 1999.

Boff, Leonardo. *Jesucristo y nuestro futuro de liberacion.* Bogotá: Indo-American Press Service, 1978.

―――. *El destino del hombre y del mundo.* Santander: Editorial Sal Terrae, 1980.

―――, and Virgil Elizondo, eds. *The People of God amidst the Poor.* Edinburgh: T&T Clark, 1984.

―――. *Faith on the Edge: Religion and Marginalized Existence.* San Franscisco: Harper & Row, 1989.

Brennan, Geoffrey H., and A. M. C. Waterman, eds. *Economics and Religion: Are They Distinct?* Dordrecht: Kluwer, 1994.

Buchanan, Allen. *Ethics, Efficiency, and the Market.* Totowa, NJ: Rowman & Allanheld, 1985.

Buchanan, James B. "The Political Economy of Franchise in the Welfare State." In Selden 1975 (below).

―――. "Markets, States, and the Extent of Morals." *American Economic Review* 62, no. 2: 364-68.

Camenisch, Paul F. "Recent Mainline Protestant Statements on Economic Justice." In *The Annual of the Society of Christian Ethics.* Knoxville: The Society of Christian Ethics, 1987.

Carlson-Thies, Stanley W., and James W. Skillen, eds. *Welfare in America: Christian Perspectives on a Policy in Crisis.* Grand Rapids: Eerdmans, 1996.

Catherwook, Frederick. "Christian Faith and Economics." *Transformation* 4, nos. 3-4 (1987): 1-84.

Cauthen, Kenneth. "Process Philosophy and the Social Order: A Freedom-Equality Model." In *Economic Life*. Chicago: Center for the Scientific Study of Religion, 1988: 89-125.

Chatterji, Saral K. "Globalisation, Structural Change, and Justice" (paper presented at 18th Biennial Council Meeting of CISRS, Calcutta, Apr. 1994). *Religion and Society* (Bangalore) 41 (June 1994): 1-61.

Childs, James M. *Greed: Economics and Ethics in Conflict*. Minneapolis: Augsburg/Fortress, 2000.

Chomsky, Noam. "How Bad Is It?" *Witness* 77 (May 1994): 8-9.

Clark, J. M. "Aims of Economic Life as Seen by Economists." Reprinted in Clark, *Economic Institutions and Human Welfare*. New York: Knopf, 1957.

Cleary, Edward, ed. *Path from Puebla: Significant Documents of the Latin American Bishops since 1979*. Trans. Phillip Berryman. Washington: National Conference of Catholic Bishops, 1989.

Clouse, Robert G., ed. *Wealth and Poverty: Four Christian Views of Economics*. Downers Grove: InterVarsity Press, 1984.

Cobb, John B. "Against Free Trade: A Meeting of Opposites." *Christian Century* 115 (Oct. 28, 1998): 999-1002.

———. "Ethics, Economics, and Free Trade." *Perspectives* 6 (Feb. 1991): 12-15.

———. "Christianity, Political Theology, and the Economic Future." In *Civil Religion and Political Theology*. South Bend: University of Notre Dame Press, 1986: 207-23.

Conferencia Nacional dos Bispos do Brasil. "Documento de los obispos Brasilenos: reflexion cristiana sobre la coyuntura politica." *Cristianismo y Sociedad* 19, nos. 3-4 (1981): 67-71.

Cook, William. "Spirituality in the Struggles for Social Justice: A Brief Latin American Anthology." *Missiology* 12 (April 1984): 223-32.

Cormie, Lee. "The Economic Crisis Is a Moral Crisis." In *Justice as Mission*. Burlington, VT: Trinity, 1985: 183-95.

Copp, D. "The Right to an Adequate Standard of Living: Justice, Autonomy, and the Basic Needs." *Social Philosophy and Policy* 9, no. 1 (Winter 1992): 213-61.

Cortes, Ernesto. "Remaining Faithful to the Vision: Dealing with the Tension between Doing Good and Doing Justice." *Church and Society* 83 (May-June 1993): 25-34.

Crowley, Michael, ed. "Toward a Christian Economic Ethic." *Epiphany* 12 (Winter 1992): 5-20, 30-33.

―――. "The Cry of the People: Asian Perspective on Reformed Faith and Economic Justice." *Reformed World* 45 (Sept. 1995): 125-36.

Daly, H., and J. Cobb. *For the Common Good: Redirecting the Economy toward Community, the Environment, and a Sustainable Future.* Boston: Beacon Press, 2d ed. 1994.

Davidson, James D., and Ralph E. Pyle. "Public Religion and Economic Inequality." In *The Power of Religious Publics.* Westport, CN: Religion in the Age of Transformation, n.d.: 101-14, 209-13.

Davis, J. B., and E. O'Boyle, eds. *The Social Economics of Human Material Need.* Carbondale: Southern Illinois University Press, 1994.

Dean, James D., and A. M. C. Waterman, eds. *Religion and Economics: Normative Social Theory.* Dordrecht: Kluwer, 1999.

De Jouvenel, Bertrand. *The Ethics of Redistribution.* Indianapolis: Liberty Fund, 1990.

DeKoster, Lester. *All Ye That Labor: An Essay on Christianity, Communism, and the Problem of Evil.* Grand Rapids: Eerdmans, 1956.

Des Jordins, Joseph R., and Barbara E. Wall, eds. "Economic Justice and Economic Rights." *Journal for Peace and Justice Studies* 1, no. 2 (1989): 1-92.

DeSoto, Hernando. *The Mystery of Capital: Why Capitalism Triumphs in the West and Fails Everywhere Else.* New York: Basic, 2000.

Douglass, Gordon K. "The Globalization of Economic Life: Economic Borders Are Erased to Allow Goods and Money to Flow Freely: Another Challenge to Justice Policies." *Church and Society* 90 (Nov.-Dec. 1999): 35-46.

Ellerman, David P. *Intellectual Trespassing as a Way of Life: Essays in Philosophy, Economics, and Mathematics.* London: Rowman & Littlefield, 1995.

Emmett, Ross B. "Frank Knight: Economics versus Religion." In H. Geoffrey Brennan and A. M. C. Watgerman: *Economics and Religion.* Dordrecht: Kluwer, 1994: 103-20.

Estrella, Julia, and Walden Bello. "Third World Perspectives: A View from below." In *A Cry for Justice.* New York: Paulist, 1989.

Etzioni, A. *The Moral Dimension: Toward a New Economics.* New York: The Free Press, 1988.

Ewert, Norm. "Justice, Charity, and Mennonite Economics." In *Anabaptist/Mennonite Faith and Economics.* Lanham, MD: University Press of America, 1994: 305-20.

Finn, Daniel Rush. "Poverty and Prosperity in Global Economics: Making Sense of Conflicting Claims." In *To Do Justice and Right upon the Earth.* Collegeville, MN: Liturgical Press, 1993: 96-105.

―――. "Ethical Dimensions of the Debate on Economic Planning." In

Catholic Social Teaching and the United States Economy. Washington, DC: University Press of America, 1984: 399-443.

―――. "International Trade and Sustainable Community: Religious Values and Economic Arguments in Moral Debates." *Journal of Religious Ethics* 22 (Fall 1994): 213-73.

―――. "The Ethical Orientations of Schools of Economic Thought." In *The Annual of the Society of Christian Ethics.* Dallas, 1982: 253-72.

Finnin, William M., and Gerald Alonzo Smith, eds. *The Morality of Scarcity: Limited Resources and Social Policy.* Baton Rouge: Louisiana State University Press, 1979.

Fishkin, James S. "The Complexity of Simple Justice." *Ethics* 98 (Apr. 1988): 464-81.

Friedman, Milton and Rose D. *Capitalism and Freedom.* Chicago: University of Chicago Press, 1962.

―――. *Free to Choose: A Personal Statement.* New York: Harcourt, Brace Jovanovich, 1980.

―――. *Politics and Tyranny.* Ed. David J. Theroux. San Francisco: Pacific Institute for Public Policy Research, 1984.

Forrester, Duncan B., and Danus Skene. *Just Sharing.* London: Epworth, 1988.

Gaiser, Frederick J. "Economics and Justice." *Word & World* 12 (Fall 1992): 319-401.

Gamwell, Franklin I. "Freedom and the Economic Order: A Foreword to Religious Evaluation." In *Christianity and Capitalism.* Chicago: Center for the Scientific Study of Religion, 1986: 49-65.

Goetz, Dieter. "De Medellín a Puebla: la evolucion de las ideas integracionistas del CELAM." *America Indigena* 44, no. 1 (Jan.-Mar. 1984): 157-81.

Goetz, Richard F. "Theological Anthropology, Self-interest, and Economic Justice in Contemporary Protestant Critiques of Capitalism." Diss., Marquette University, 1998.

Gorringe, Timothy J. *Capital and the Kingdom: Theological Ethics and Economic Order.* New York: Orbis, 1994.

Gottwald, Norman K. "From Biblical Economies to Modern Economies: A Bridge over Troubled Waters." In *Churches in Struggle.* New York: Monthly Review Press, 1986: 138-48.

Goudzwaard, Bob. "Freedom and Justice: Evangelical Responsibilities in Politics and the Economy." *Epworth Review* 19 (Sept. 1992): 242-31.

―――. *Capitalism and Progress.* Trans. Josina Van Nuis Zylstra. Toronto: Wedge, 1979.

Goulet, Denis. "Goals in Conflict: Corporate Success and Global Justice."

In *The Judeo-Christian Vision and the Modern Corporation.* Notre Dame: University of Notre Dame Press, 1982: 218-47.

―――. "Economic Systems, Middle Way Theories, and Third World Realities." In *Co-creation and Capitalism.* Washington, DC: University Press of America, 1983: 141-69.

Gower, Joseph F., ed. *Religion and Economic Ethics.* Lanham, MD: University Press of America, 1990 (Annual Publication of the College Theological Society 31).

Graham, Gordon. "Justice, Charity, and the Third World." *Modern Theology* 3, no. 1 (Oct. 1986): 21-33.

Gregorios, Paulos. "Justice among Nations: The Struggle for a Just International Economic Order." In *Religious Workers for Lasting Peace Disarmament and Just relations among Nations.* Moscow: Department of External Church Relations, Moscow Patriarchy, 1978: 73-84.

Griffiths, Brian. "The Conservative Quadrilateral: Christian Values and a Market Economy." In *Christianity and Conservatism.* London: Hodder & Stoughton, 1990: 217-41.

Gronbacher, Gregory M. A. *Economic Personalism: A New Paradigm for a Humane Economy.* Grand Rapids: Acton Institute Occasional Paper #10, 1998.

Gunneman, Jon P. "The Circumstances of Economic Justice: A Response to Kenneth Cauthen." In *Economic Life.* Chicago: Center for the Scientific Study of Religion, 1988: 127-40.

―――. "Capital Ideas: Theology Engages the Economic." *Religion and Values in Public Life* (Harvard Divinity Bulletin) 7 (Fall 1998): 5-8.

―――. "Thinking Theologically about the Economic." In *Christian Ethics.* Cleveland: Pilgrim, 1996: 315-33.

Haan, Roelf L. "Man and Methodology in Economic Science." In *Social Science in Christian Perspective.* Lanham, MD: University Press of America, 1988: 219-66.

Hamlin, A. P. *Ethics, Economics, and the State.* New York: St. Martin's, 1986.

Haslett, David W. *Capitalism with Morality.* Oxford: Oxford University Press, 1994.

Hausman, D. M., and M. S. McPherson. *Economic Analysis and Moral Philosophy.* Cambridge: Cambridge University Press, 1996.

Hawtrey, Kim. "Economic Justice: A Twin Axiom Framework." *Reformed Theological Review* 50 (Sept.-Dec. 1991): 98-105.

Hay, Donald A. *Economics Today: A Christian Critique.* Grand Rapids: Eerdmans, 1989.

―――. "What Does the Lord Require? Three Statements on Christian Faith and Economic Life." *Transformation* 10 (Jan.-Apr. 1993): 10-15.

Hedlund, Roger E. "Christian Freedom and Third World Realities." In *Christian Freedom*. Lanham, MD: University Press of America, 1986: 217-33.

Heilbronner, Robert L. *The Worldly Philosophers*. New York: Simon and Schuster, 1967.

———. *The Nature and Logic of Capitalism*. New York: W. W. Norton, 1985.

———. *The Essential Adam Smith*. New York: W. W. Norton, 1986.

Hendrickson, Mark W., ed. *The Morality of Capitalism*. New York: The Foundation for Economic Education, 1996.

Henriot, Peter J. "The Challenge of Global Prosperity: Social Justice and Solidarity." *Journal of Ecumenical Studies* 24 (Summer 1987): 382-93.

———. "Wealth, Poverty, Hunger: The Ethics of the International Economic Order." In *Called to Love*. Villanova: Villanova University Press, 1985: 97-125.

Heschel, Abraham J. *The Prophets*. New York: Harper Torchbooks, 1962.

Heyn, H. *The Economic Way of Thinking*. Chicago: SRA Inc., 2d ed. 1976.

Heyne, Paul. *Religion and Economics*. Dordrecht: Kluwer Academic Publications, 1999.

Hicks, Douglas A. *Inequality and Christian Ethics*. Cambridge: Cambridge University Press, 2000.

Hinkelammert, Franz J. *The Ideological Weapons of Death: A Theological Critique of Capitalism*. Trans. Phillip Berryman. Maryknoll, NY: Orbis, 1986.

Hirschman, A. O. "Rival Interpretations of Market Society: Civilizing, Destructive, or Feeble," *Journal of Economic Literature* 20. (Dec. 1982): 1463-84.

———. *The Passions and the Interests*. Princeton: Princeton University Press, 1977.

Hoch, Lothar. "Economia Mundial e Ausencia De Justica: Questionamento na Perspectiva do Terceiro Mundo." *Estudios Teologicos* 34, no. 3 (1994): 282-90.

Jeune, Chavannes. "Justice, Freedom and Social Transformation." In *The Church in Response to Human Need*. Monrovia: Missions Advanced Research and Communication Center, 1983: 329-42.

Johnson, Luke Timothy. *Sharing Possessions: Mandate and Symbol of Faith*. Philadelphia: Fortress, 1981.

Johnson, Paul. "The Capitalism and Morality Debate." *First Things* 1 (Mar. 1990): 18-22.

Jordan, B. *The Common Good: Citizenship, Morality, and Self-Interest*. New York: Basil Blackwell, 1989.

Keller, Jack A. "Hunger and Multinational Corporations: An Ethical Analysis." *Saint Luke's Journal of Theology* 26 (Spring 1983): 285-311.

Kerr, Shirley. "Morality and Faith from a First World–Third World Perspective." *Religious Education* 80 (Spring 1985): 173-93.

Korten, David C. *When Corporations Rule the World.* West Hartford, CN: Kumarian, 1995.

Krueger, David A. "Capitalism, Christianity, and Economic Ethics: An Illustrative Survey of Twentieth-century Protestant Social Ethics." In *Christianity and Capitalism.* Chicago: Center for the Scientific Study of Religion, 1986: 25-45.

Kuthner, R. *Everything for Sale: The Virtues and Limits of Markets.* New York: Alfred Knopf, 1997.

Kuyper, Abraham. *The Problem of Poverty.* Ed. James W. Skillen. Grand Rapids: Baker, 1991.

————. *Lectures on Calvinism.* Grand Rapids: Eerdmans, 1978.

Lebacqz, Karen. *Six Theories of Justice.* Minneapolis: Augsburg, 1986.

Lerner, Michael, ed. "Prophets vs. Profits: Meaning in the Marketplace." *Tikkun* 11 (May-June 1996): 13-20, 25-32, 54-55, 79.

Lindblom, Charles E. *Politics and Markets: The World's Political Economic Systems.* New York: Basic Books, 1977.

Lizano, Eduardo, Roberto Murillo, and Mose Miguel Rodriguez, eds. "Politica economica, etica social y espiritualidad." *Para el Debate* (Mayo 1991). Heredia, Costa Rica.

Llach, Juan. Desarrollo Economic y Justicia Social en America Latina: Ideas para una Esperanza." In *Desafios a la doctrina social de la iglesia en America Latina.* Bogotá: Consejo Episcopal Latinoamericano, 1985: 269-310.

Long, Edward LeRoy. "Christian Ethics as Responses to Social Conditions." In *Altered Landscapes.* Grand Rapids: Eerdmans, 1989: 296-311.

Long, Stephen D. *Divine Economy: Theology and the Market.* London: Routledge, 2000.

Lovin, Robin W. "Self-sufficiency or Equitable Development: Moral Issues in World Food Policy." *Religious Studies Review* 7 (Oct. 1981): 328-32.

Lutz, Charles P., ed. *God, Goods and the Common Good: Eleven Perspectives on Economic Justice in Dialogue with the Roman Catholic Bishop's Pastoral Letter.* Minneapolis: Augsburg, 1987.

Lutz, Mark A. *Economics for the Common Good: Two Centuries of Social Economic Thought in the Humanistic Tradition.* London: Routledge, 1999.

————, and Kenneth Lux. *The Challenge of Humanistic Economics.* Menlo Park, NJ: Benjamin Cummings, 1979.

MacPherson, C. B. *The Political Economy of Possessive Individualism: Hobbes to Locke.* Oxford: Oxford University Press, 1962.

————. *The Rise and Fall of Economic Justice and Other Papers*. Oxford: Oxford University Press, 1985.

Maguire, Daniel C. *The Moral Core of Judaism and Christianity*. Minneapolis: Fortress, 1993.

————. *A New American Justice*. New York: Doubleday, 1980.

Mara, Gerald. "Poverty and Justice: the Bishops and Contemporary Liberalism." In *The Deeper Meaning of Economic Life*. Washington: Georgetown University Press, 1986: 157-78.

Marshall, Paul. "A Christian View of Economics." *Crux* 21, no. 1 (Mar. 1985): 3-6.

Mason, John R. "Seven Theses toward an Ecumenical Economic Ethic for the 1990s." *Pro Ecclesia* 3 (Winter 1994): 68-88.

McCann, Dennis P. "The Shape of Economic Justice in the 21st Century." Review of R. B. Reich, *The Work of Nations*. *Christian Century* 108 (Oct. 30, 1991): 1003-8.

————. "Liberation and the Multinationals." *Theology Today* 41 (Apr. 1984): 51-60.

McPherson, Michael S. "Want Formation, Morality, and Some Interpretive Aspects of Economic Inquiry." In *Social Science as Moral Inquiry*. New York: Columbia University Press, 1983: 96-124.

Meeks, M. Douglas. *God the Economist: The Doctrine of God and Political Economy*. Minneapolis: Fortress, 1989.

Mendez, Guillermo W. "El sustrato teologico de la Economia." Paper presented at Fe Cristiana y Economia Conference of the Fraternidad Teologica Latinoamericana, Antigua, Guatemala, Ag 26-29, 1993. *Kairos* 13 (July-Dec. 1993): 25-46.

Mieth, Dietmar, and Marciano Vidal, eds. *Outside the Market: No Salvation*. London: SCM, 1997.

————, and Jacques Pohier, eds. *Christian Ethics and Economics: The North-South Conflict*. New York: Seabury, 1980.

Mill, John S. *Principles of Political Economy with Some of Their Applications to Social Philosophy*, vols. 1 and 2. New York: D. Appleton, 1891.

Miller, David. "Distributive Justice: What the People Think." *Ethics* 102 (Apr. 1992): 555-93.

National Conference of Catholic Bishops. *Economic Justice for All*. Washington, DC, 1986.

Novak, Michael. *The Spirit of Democratic Capitalism*. New York: Simon & Schuster, 1982.

————. "Political Economy and Christian Conscience" (reply to J. P. Wogaman [below], 523-28). *Journal of Ecumenical Studies* 24 (Summer 1987): 394-402.

————. "The Future of Economic Rights." In *Private Virtue and Public Policy.* New Brunswick, NJ: Transaction, 1990: 69-81.

————. "Wealth and Virtue: The Development of Christian Economic Teaching." In *The Capitalist Spirit.* San Francisco: ICS Press, 1990: 51-80.

————. "Defining Social Justice." *First Things* 108 (Dec. 2000): 11-13.

Owensby, Walter L. *Economics for Prophets.* Grand Rapids: Eerdmans, 1988.

Ortega, Ofelia. "The Word That Inspires and Upholds in the Struggle for Justice: A Latin American Perspective." *Reformed World* 44 (Mar. 1994): 28-38.

Palanca, Ellen H. "Religion and Economic Development." In *God and Global Justice.* New York: Paragon, 1985: 65-83.

Parel, Anthony, and Thomas Flanagan, eds. *Theories of Property: Aristotle to the Present.* Waterloo: Wilfrid Laurier University Press, 1979.

Parker, Cristian G. ed. "Etica y desarrollo: desafio para America Latina." *Cristianismo y Sociedad* 33, nos. 3-4 (1995): 1-167.

Parker, Paul P. *Standing with the Poor: Theological Reflections on Economic Reality.* Cleveland: Pilgrim, 1992.

Parker, Richard. "Becoming Evangelists of Justice: What Will It Take to Build a Humane Global Economy?" *Sojourners* 28 (Sept.-Oct. 1999): 36-39.

Paul, Ellen Frankel, Fred D. Miller, and Jeffrey Paul, eds. *Ethics and Economics.* Oxford: Basil Blackwell, 1985.

Pawlikowski, John T. "A Growing Tradition of Ethical Critique: A Bibliography." In *Economic Justice.* Washington: Pastoral Press, 1988: 39-48.

Peck, Jane Carey. "Reflections from Costa Rica on Protestantism's Dependence and Nonliberative Social Function." *Journal of Ecumenical Studies* 21 (Spring 1984): 181-98.

Pemberton, Prentiss. "Lockian Liberalism: A Radical Shift from the Biblical Economic Ethic." In *In the Great Tradition.* Valley Forge, PA: Judson, 1982: 107-19.

Powelson, John P. "Holistic Economics." *Theology Today* 41 (Apr. 1984): 66-77.

Ranck, Lee, ed. "Faith and Economic Justice." *Christian Social Action* 4 (Sept. 1991): 4-16, 25-34.

Rawlings, Charles W. "Social Justice and the Economic Crisis: Route Markets to the New Exodus." *Church and Society* 73, no. 5 (May-June 1983): 42-52.

Rayack, Elton. *Not So Free to Choose: The Political Economy of Milton Friedman and Ronald Reagan.* New York: Praeger, 1987.

Richardson, James T., and David G. Bromley. "Religion, Economics, and Society." *Sociological Analysis* 49 (Dec. 1988): 1-95.

Rieger, Jeorg, ed. *Liberating the Future: God, Mammon, and Theology.* Minneapolis: Augsburg/Fortress, 1998.

Rima, Ingrid Hahne. *The Development of Economic Analysis.* London: Routledge, 1996.

Rooy, Sidney. "Righteousness and Justice." *Evangelical Review of Theology* 6, no. 2 (Oct. 1982): 260-74.

Rubenstein, Richard L. "Religion, Ideology, and Economic Justice." In *The Terrible Meek.* New York: Paragon, 1987: 169-88.

Samandu, Luis, and Hans Siebers. "The Struggle for Life within the Central American Society in Crisis." *Exchange* 15, nos. 43-44 (Apr.-Sept. 1986): 7-50.

Santa Ana, Julio de. "The Rights to Development and Economic Justice." *Reformed World* 48 (Sept. 1998): 120-30.

Schafer, Klaus, ed. "God and Mammon: Economies in Conflict." *Mission Studies* 13, nos. 1-2 (1996): 10-369.

Schlossberg, Herbert, Vinay Samuel, and Ronald Sider, eds. *Christianity and Economics in the Post–Cold War Era: The Oxford Declaration and Beyond.* Grand Rapids: Eerdmans, 1994.

Schroeder, William Widick. "American Democratic Capitalism: A Sympathetic Appraisal." In *Liberation and Ethics.* Chicago: Center for the Scientific Study of Religion, 1985: 145-58.

Schrotenboer, Paul G., et al. *And He Had Compassion on Them.* Grand Rapids: Board of Publications of the Christian Reformed Church, 1978.

———. "Calvin on Interest and Property — Some Aspects of His Socio-Economic view." In *Our Reformed Tradition.* Potchefstroom: Institute for Reformational Studies, 1984: 217-30.

Sedgwick, Peter H. *The Market Economy and Christian Ethics.* Cambridge: Cambridge University Press, 1999.

Selden, Richard T. *Capitalism and Freedom: Problems and Prospects, Proceedings of a Conference in Honor of Milton Friedman.* Charlottesville, VA: University Press of Virginia, 1975.

Sen, Amartya. *On Ethics and Economics.* Oxford: Basil Blackwell, 1987.

———. "The Moral Standing of the Market." In *Ethics and Economics.* Ed. Ellen Frankel Paul, Fred D. Miller Jr., and Jeffrey Paul. Oxford: Basil Blackwell, 1985.

Sider, Ron. *Just Generosity: A New Vision for Overcoming Poverty in America.* Grand Rapids: Baker, 1999.

Smurl, James F. "Common Moral and Religious Grounds for Uncommon Economic Times." In *Religion and Economic Ethics.* Lanham, MD: University Press of America, 1990.

Sobrino, Jon. "Unjust and Violent Poverty in Latin America." In *Council for Peace*. Edinburgh: T&T Clark, 1988: 55-60.

Solle, Dorothee. "Justice Is the True Name of Peace." *Church and Society* 73, no. 5 (May-June 1983): 14-22.

Stackhouse, Max L. *Christian Social Ethics in a Global Era*. Nashville: Abingdon, 1995.

————. *Public Theology and Political Economy*. Grand Rapids: Eerdmans, 1987.

————. "What Then Shall We Do? On Using Scripture in Economic Ethics." *Interpretation* 41 (Oct. 1987): 382-97.

Stivers, Robert L., ed. *Reformed Faith and Economics*. Lanham, MD: University Press of America, 1989.

Strain, Charles R., ed. *Prophetic Visions and Economic Realities: Protestants, Jews, and Catholics Confront the Bishop's Letter on the Economy*. Grand Rapids: Eerdmans, 1989.

Sturm, Douglas. "Economic Justice and the Commonwealth of Peoples." In *Religion and Economic Ethics*. Lanham, MD: University Press of America, 1990.

Tawney, R. H. *Religion and the Rise of Capitalism*. New York: Harcourt, Brace, 1926.

Tiemstra, John P. "Science, Information and Valued." *Perspectives* 10 (Aug.-Sept. 1995): 3-4.

————, ed. *Reforming Economics*. Lewiston: Edwin Mellen, 1990.

Trimiew, Darryl M. "The Economic Rights Debate: The End of One Argument, the Beginning of Another." In *The Annual of the Society of Christian Ethics*. Washington: Georgetown University Press, 1991: 85-108.

Uko, Hans, ed. *The Jubilee Challenge: Utopia or Possibility?* Geneva: WCC Publications, 1977.

Vandezande, Gerald. "Faith and Justice, Poverty and Unemployment: How Do They Relate and What Can We Do?" *ARC* 26 (1998): 111-24.

Vander Heide, Evert. "Justice in International Economic Relations with Less Developed Countries." *Transformation* 1, no. 2 (Apr.-June 1984): 2-8.

Van Drimmelen, Rob. *Faith in a Global Economy*. Geneva: WCC Publications, 1998.

Van Dyk, Harry. "How Abraham Kuyper Became a Christian Democrat." *Calvin Theological Journal* 33 (Nov. 1998): 420-35.

Wadell, Paul J. "The Common Good: Why There Can Be No Justice without It." In *Economic Justice*. Washington: Pastoral Press, 1988: 57-64.

Walters, Stanley D. "Review Symposium on Christian Faith and Economic Justice." *Toronto Journal of Theology* 7 (Spring 1991): 19-57.

Walzer, Michael. *Spheres of Justice: A Defense of Pluralism and Equality.* New York: Basic, 1983.

———, and David Miller. *Pluralism, Justice, and Equality.* Oxford: Oxford University Press, 1995.

Williams, Oliver F., and John W. Houck, eds. *The Common Good and US Capitalism.* Lanham, MD: University Press of America, 1987.

Wilson, John Oliver. "Economic Justice and Corporate America: Response to Catholic and Protestant Economic Statements." In *Cry for Justice.* New York: Paulist, 1989: 81-93.

Wogaman, J. Philip. *Economics and Ethics: A Christian Inquiry.* Philadelphia: Fortress, 1986.

———. "The Theological Context of Economic Policy." *Engage/Social Action* 10 (May 1982): 30-35.

———. "Emerging Issues in Economic Ethics." In *The Annual of the Society of Christian Ethics.* Washington, DC: Georgetown University Press, 1984: 93-121.

Wolterstorff, Nicholas. *Till Justice and Peace Embrace.* Grand Rapids: Eerdmans, 1998.

Wortman, Julie A. "Economic Justice or Charity: The Episcopalian Church and Community Development." *Witness* 75 (Mar. 1992): 16-18.

Wuthnow, Robert. *God and Mammon in America.* New York: The Free Press/Toronto: Maxwell Macmillan, 1994.

———, ed. *Rethinking Materialism: Perspective on the Spiritual Dimension of Economic Behavior.* Grand Rapids: Eerdmans, 1995.

Yoder, John H. "The Conditions of Countercultural Credibility." In *The Making of an Economic Vision: John Paul II's On social concern.* Lanham, MD: University Press of America, 1991: 261-74.

Young, H. Peyton. *Equity.* Princeton: Princeton University Press, 1994.

Zweig, Michael, ed. *Religion and Economic Justice.* Philadelphia: Temple University Press, 1991.

Index of Names

Index of Subjects

Index of Scripture References

INDEX OF SCRIPTURE REFERENCES

LINCOLN CHRISTIAN UNIVERSITY

LaVergne, TN USA
09 January 2011
211722LV00009B/79/P

3 4711 00207 6588